# NOIKE

A MEMOIR of LEON GINSBURG

*One Boy's Remarkable Journey of Survival
Through the Holocaust*

written by SUZANNE GINSBURG

# NOIKE

Noike : A Memoir of Leon Ginsburg, One Boy's Remarkable Journey of Survival Through the Holocaust by Suzanne Ginsburg

Copyright © 2012 by Suzanne Ginsburg
Photography copyright © 2012 Leon Ginsburg

All rights reserved. Except for brief passages quoted in newspaper, magazine, radio, television or online reviews, no part of this book may be reproduced in any form by any means, electronic or mechanical, including photocopying, recording or information storage or retrieval system without permission in writing from the author.

Published in the United States by Avenger Books
22 Liberty Street
San Francisco, CA 94110

www.noikethebook.com

Printed in the United States
Cover design: Nicole Celichowski

First Edition
10 9 8 7 6 5 4 3 2 1

ISBN: 978-0-615-56199-8

Library of Congress Cataloging-in-Publication Data
Library of Congress Control Number: 2012900347

Ginsburg, Suzanne
   Noike : A Memoir of Leon Ginsburg, One Boy's Remarkable Journey of Survival Through the Holocaust
/ Suzanne Ginsburg

*For Pesel, Blima, and Herschel*

# 1

# LITTLE BOY MEETS GIRL

*New York ~ San Francisco ~ Florida*

"Your dad looks great," my father's friend said, stabbing his fork into a hunk of noodle pudding. My older sister had purchased all of my dad's favorite foods—noodle pudding, *knishes, pierogis*—for his birthday party at her house on Long Island. With my brother living in London and me in San Francisco, she had become the de facto family hostess in recent years.

"I know—I can't believe he's 70!" I replied. We both paused to take in the figure my father cut on the other side of the room, where he was telling a story to a few old friends from City College with his usual, animated flourish. My mother, sister, brother, nieces, nephews, and dozens of other guests were scattered throughout the house and backyard.

"He's like Dick Clark," my father's friend continued, swallowing his last bite of noodle pudding. "One day he'll suddenly get old—"

Forcing a smile, I picked up a mini-*knish* and stuffed it into my mouth. *And die*, I thought, completing his sentence in my head. My father's friend didn't mean any harm but his words were unsettling. *He's going to get old and die, right?*

I'm not a morbid person. It had been almost ten years since I had contemplated my dad's mortality during a drive to Newark airport. I had been in New York for a few weeks and was heading back to Japan, where I lived and worked for three years in the early-1990s. We were somewhere on the New Jersey Turnpike when a horrible scene started playing in my head: What if my dad had less than 24 hours to live? Even if I jumped on the first plane out of Japan, I might not make it home in time. I imagined rushing into the hospital room and the nurse saying, "Sorry, honey, you just missed him." By the time we arrived at the airport I had become fixated on this scenario. Unable to share my morbid thoughts, I burst into tears and blurted: "I'm going to miss you!" My father was stunned; I never cried when saying goodbye. "I'll see you soon," he smiled, wiping my tears with a tissue.

Standing there at my dad's 70th birthday, I had that same sick feeling, like I might lose him at any moment. San Francisco was closer than Japan, but it was still more than five hours by plane. Part of me knew that I was being dramatic, maybe even perversely grim, but I didn't want to be one of those people that you see in the movies— slumped over a dead loved one, wishing they had said or done something meaningful for the deceased when they had the chance.

Later that evening, after most of the guests had gone home, my father started thumbing through a photo album that was assembled over the course of the party. In lieu of gifts—which my father never wanted–each guest was asked to bring a photo, with the only specification being that the image should resonate with my father in some way.

"Ho, ho, ho!" my father said as he looked at the first page. "Who are these gorgeous children?" He turned the album around and showed off a collage of his six grandchildren.

"That's us, *Zeidi*!" Isabel said, climbing onto his lap. She was three years old, the youngest grandchild.

"And who's this pretty little girl?" he asked, looking over at me.

He held up a page that bore a photo of us from New York, circa 1976. In it I'm wearing a short, checkered green dress and smiling for the camera; my father is standing over me in a floral button-down shirt and blue jeans. I was very much Daddy's little girl back then, always running down the hallway when I saw his car pull into the driveway, eager to wrap my arms around his neck. I can still remember his soft brown hair tickling my eyes and nose as he hugged me, the feeling of relief when he finally walked through the door at night.

I can't say how that photo resonated with my father, but for me it called up powerful memories of our storytelling ritual during that period. Every night my father would sit beside me and tell me about a little boy who roamed the farms and forests of a faraway place, befriending foxes, dogs, and sheep. The stories were never scary, but they suggested mystery, and were tinged with the darkness of a certain kind of children's fable. In one story, the little boy was sleeping in a haystack when a farmer poked him with a pitchfork. He wasn't harmed but I wondered: Where were the boy's father and mother? Why was he alone? At some point I realized that the young boy was in fact my father, but between us passed a kind of tacit agreement to keep his identity secret, to let him remain in the faraway forest. Like the homeless little boy, I knew my father had also lost his family; unlike the rest of my friends, I never had a full set of aunts, uncles, and grandparents.

The stories stopped when I became too old to be tucked into bed, or maybe it was when I started watching television with my mother. Unlike most families, our primary television—the only one without static—was in the master bedroom. My dad would sit in the kitchen to watch the evening news on the "small" TV, occasionally poking his head into the bedroom. "Who wants dessert?" he would ask my mother and I as we lay on the bed, transfixed by the latest *Dynasty* cliffhanger. "Not now, not now," we would say, afraid of missing some critical part of the story. "What could be so important?" he'd ask, then leave the room with an incredulous shake of his head. A short time later he would return with some elaborate combination of ice cream, cookies, and cake for me, and tea for my mother, then tiptoe out once his work was done.

More than a decade later, I tried to recapture his stories within the confines of a college writing assignment. By then I knew that my father's family had been killed in Poland, during the Holocaust, but I didn't know exactly when or how. He had agreed to help me with some research for the assignment, and I remember sitting on the living room couch for several hours as he lectured me on the commerce, utilities, and transportation systems in his small Polish town. Not once did he mention my grandparents, aunts, uncles, or cousins; not once did he mention the war. I now see how naïve I had been: How could I have expected him to tell me—his innocent eighteen-year-old daughter—about the horrors he and his family had experienced?

When I returned to San Francisco after my dad's 70th birthday, I kept thinking about his stories and the prediction made by his friend: *He's going to suddenly get old.* Those words were a painful reminder that my father would not always be here to share his memories, to provide a window into the lost world of my aunts, uncles, grandparents, and great-grandparents. Flashing forward to the future, I imagined myself alone in his office, rifling through his reams of notes and old photographs with so many questions, wishing I had asked them long ago. The answers would remain trapped in his mind, his descendants left with only a vague understanding of what he had experienced.

I realized that I needed to find out what happened, right then, before it was too late. Not knowing where or how to begin, I enrolled in several writing classes and immersed myself in biographies, memoirs, and Holocaust history books. As I gained confidence, I started thinking about the logistics: Could I write his stories on nights and weekends? Should I request a sabbatical from my job? And then it came to me: I had to quit my job and focus on his stories. Without a full commitment, it would end up just like my college writing assignment—a few interesting historical facts but not the *real* story. I had been saving money for a down-payment on an apartment; it was more than enough to support me for one year. The apartment in San Francisco could wait.

When I finally shared my plans with my father, I was expecting a long discussion full of awkward silences, but he simply said: "I always knew you would do it." It was as if the date and time were marked on his calendar; it was as if he had been sitting there, waiting for my phone call. His response made me feel like I was doing the right thing, that maybe I was *meant* to do this in some weird, spiritual way. I pictured the homeless little boy racing through the forest, joyful that his stories would finally be told.

About two months later, I flew from San Francisco to Florida, where my parents had recently retired. I planned to spend the entire four days interviewing my father, starting from the beginning. I had no idea how far we'd get, but felt we now had enough time not to worry: I had already quit my job; this was my number one priority.

"So, what do you want to do while you're here?" my father asked as we drove from West Palm Beach airport to their home in nearby Boynton Beach. "Your mother said you might like Morikami Gardens or the bird sanctuary—they're only about 30 minutes away. And of course there's the pool and beach!"

"They all sound fun but I want to work on your stories," I said, confused by the sightseeing suggestions. "Unless you changed your mind?"

"No, no, that's good," he said, lowering the radio. "I have *all* my papers organized for you!" He proceeded to list all of the maps, photos, and news clippings he had arranged in manila folders for my visit.

"Great, I can't wait to see what you have," I said, relieved that he, too, was serious about the interviews. I pictured him proudly telling all of his friends: *My daughter is writing a book about me! Quit her job and everything. Can you believe it?* It was probably the only time a Jewish parent could justifiably brag about their child not having a job.

At the entrance to their community my father clicked the remote control that lifts the gate, allowing us inside. We passed a large fountain, wound our way along the main road, then turned down my parents' street. From the outside, their house looks like most of the others on the block: one level, light stucco exterior, red tile roof. The houses are spaced fairly close together, but many of the neighbors don't know each other. A large number of the residents still work full time while others are "snow birds"—winter residents who head back up north when spring arrives.

"Betty, your daughter is here!" my father called as we entered the house.

"Did you miss your old mother?" my mother grinned as she approached the front door with her arms wide. Before I could reply she had begun an impromptu house tour, showing me what she had bought since my visit the previous winter. She avoided my father's office, the one room in the house she'd agreed not to decorate. What furnishings it contained were buried under assorted piles of paper: dozens of books and articles, stacks of unfinished personal stories, newspaper clippings, and countless black and white photos of people and places known only to my father.

THE NEXT MORNING MY FATHER STROLLED into the kitchen wearing one of his newly acquired Florida outfits: a yellow-and-white striped golf shirt, khaki shorts, and Rockports. "Good morning!" he said. "Your mother already left for the fashion show but she'll be back in time for dinner." Hadassah, a group for Jewish women, organizes group outings like the fashion show each month; last time the ladies saw the King Tut exhibit in Miami.

"You slept well?"

"Not bad," I replied, as I finished setting up the video camera. I planned to take hand-written notes but I wanted to make sure I didn't miss anything. The video would serve as backup.

"Look at these birds," my father said, pointing out the window. "I enjoy watching them, especially in the morning when they come to eat. It's amazing how long they can stay underneath the water."

Watching my father gaze at the birds, I realized that I had to take the lead and start asking questions. If it was up to him, we would spend the whole day reviewing Polish, Russian, and German history and the various pacts that led up to the war. Brushing up on my World War II history was critical but I was eager to immerse myself in the little boy's world, in my father's lost world. I wanted to walk in his footsteps, see what he saw in Maciejow, Poland in 1939. At the same time, I knew it was important to ease my father into the interviews. If he felt rushed or pressured, I was afraid he might shut down. Being a novice interviewer, I started with the obvious questions.

"Dad, you were born in Machiev in 1932, right?"

"Yes, but you're spelling it wrong, it's M-a-c-i-e-j-o-w," he tapped at my notebook.

"And you were called Noah back then?"

"Noah was my Hebrew name; Noike was my Polish name," he explained.

"So, when did things start to change in Maciejow?" I corrected the spelling of his hometown in my notebook.

"1939—that's when we got occupied by the Soviet Union. September 17th, 1939. You know how I remember that date?" He did not wait for a response: "Because they renamed the main street '*Sedimnazietavo Verezina. September 17th!*"

# 2

# THE RED STORM
*Maciejow, Poland. September 1939*

"Momma—the Russians are back!" Seven-year-old Noike was breathless but duty-bound as he burst into his house to report on the afternoon's events. He was known as the little *yenta*, a busybody, always providing daily updates on all of the happenings around the small Polish town of Maciejow. Once he went too far, telling the rabbi when his teenaged aunts were writing on the Sabbath—an act strictly forbidden in the Talmud. His aunts literally dove out of a first-storey window when they saw the rabbi and their five-year-old nephew walking hand-in-hand towards their secret writing place.

"Noikele, there you are," his mother, Pesel, said as she emerged from her bedroom. She was thirty-three years old with deep blue eyes and wavy brown hair, features young Noike had inherited. When her husband, Kalman, died of pneumonia six years earlier—one year after Noike was born—she became the head of the household. Noike was too young to remember his father but he would never forget how his mother described his hair: "Black as a bumblebee."

"Where's Herschel?" Noike was eager to share the latest news with his older brother. He often tagged along with Herschel when his mother was busy minding the fabric store. In recent weeks he had listened to the older boys talk about Germany, Russia, and France—places far from their simple life in Maciejow. Now these places seemed not so distant: *real* Russian soldiers were in *their* town.

"Herschel went with *Baba* and Blima to the store to pack up the rest of the fabrics," Pesel explained. *Baba* was her mother; Blima was the eldest of her three children, nearly eleven years old.

"Come, Noikele—we must get everything out before the soldiers arrive!" Pesel took Noike's hand.

Though Russian soldiers were novel to young Noike, they were only too familiar to his elders, who had witnessed past wars over the border lands. Located in a region called Eastern Volhynia, Maciejow is about 150 miles east of the former border between Poland and Soviet Union. The region had been part of Tzarist Russia but was given to Poland at the end of the First World War. Twenty years later, Stalin was claiming that the Soviet Union had invaded in order to protect its "blood brothers," but it was clear that the primary goal was to reclaim lost land.

Signs of an imminent invasion had surfaced a few weeks earlier, after refugees and wounded Polish cavalry units fled from western Poland into Maciejow. Townspeople emerged from their homes, offering the Polish soldiers bread and milk. Word later spread that the non-aggression pact between Germany and the Soviet Union, known as the Molotov-Ribbentrop Act, included a secret clause to divide Poland in the event of war. Nine days after the pact was signed, Germany invaded the western half of Poland; two weeks later the Soviet Union struck the eastern half of Poland. The Polish Army, poorly equipped to fight a one-front war, let alone a two-front war, fell within weeks.

One of the Red Army's first orders of business in Maciejow was to order all of the shopkeepers to open their stores and sell their merchandise at a nominal exchange rate: one Polish *zloty* for every Russian *ruble*. The soldiers went wild, some purchasing multiple gold watches for themselves, countless silk stockings and slips for their girlfriends. Pesel was one of the lucky merchants. She managed to smuggle most of her inventory back to their home, bundling it into the shape of a mattress and covering it with bedding. Customers who used to come to the store started coming to her home. Blima and Herschel helped cut and wrap the fabrics; Noike often greeted customers.

"*Dzien dobry*," Mrs. Shliva said as she stood in the doorway. She was carrying a basket loaded with cheese and butter. "Is your mother home, Noika?" The Poles and Ukrainians pronounced his name "Noika" instead of "Noike."

Noike nodded his head; he recognized Mrs. Shliva from the store.

"Come in, come in," Pesel said, overhearing their conversation at the door. "You wanted some fabric for your daughter's dress? Let's go to my bedroom; I have a beautiful floral print in mind."

"*Do widzenia*, Noika," Mrs. Shliva smiled as they went to Pesel's bedroom.

A FEW WEEKS INTO THE OCCUPATION, the Soviet Union sent representatives to install a Communist-style government. Only a select few—mostly Ukrainians who did not appear "too nationalistic," or Jews who did not seem "too religious" or "too capitalist"—were assigned coveted government positions. Poles would not take part in the new government. Polish elites, intellectuals, and former government officials fled town a few days before the occupation, heeding rumors that they would be arrested by the NKVD—the Soviet secret police—and exiled to Siberia.

The new Communist government shut down the few businesses that remained and put an end to the weekly *Der Markt Tag*—market day. Jews who were unable to stow away their inventories were devastated by the closures; they were the proprietors of the town's shoemaking shops, millineries, confectionaries, and most other businesses. These businesses were replaced with state-owned depots, offering only the essentials for communist life. Noike and Herschel would wait in line for hours for a loaf of bread, often returning home with nothing; the poorly operated stores were unable to adapt and keep up with the demand.

WHEN NOIKE RETURNED TO SCHOOL a few weeks later, he met his new teacher, an older Ukrainian woman as fluent in Russian as she was in communist ideology. "*Dobroye utro*," she greeted Noike in Russian as he entered the classroom, her hands clasped in front of her broad waist. Noike looked up at the new teacher, unsure how to respond to the foreign words. *Dobroye utro* sounded similar to *Dobyi den*, or "Good morning" in Ukrainian, a phrase he often heard when greeting customers at his mother's store. "*Dobroye utro*," he finally said.

The teacher smiled, then greeted the next child in the same manner.

Polish would no longer be spoken in the public schools. The Ukrainian teacher handed out the new Russian textbooks and formally introduced the class to the motherland: a huge map of the Soviet Union was displayed where the Polish one once hung. All of the students were encouraged to join the Young Pioneers, a Communist youth movement that held sports events, showed films, and organized parades. Noike eventually became a member, wearing a red scarf around his neck and waving a big red flag as he marched through town in the annual parade; not understanding the meaning of the

Soviet propaganda, he simply wanted to participate in the only activities in town. Pesel allowed her son to take part in the events—refusal would have been deemed anti-communist.

In the two years that followed, many of those who protested the government would disappear in the night, never to be seen again.

# 3

# THE BLACK STORM
*Maciejow, Poland. June 1941*

Noike pulled his pillow over his head but the bombs were relentless—more frightful than thunder and lightning, more frightful than anything that had ever woken him in the night. He went into his mother's bedroom and quietly stood near her bed. Sensing someone's presence, she opened her eyes and softly smiled at her youngest child. "Come baby, come sleep with Momma," Pesel said, placing a quilt around his ears and holding him until he fell asleep.

The German attack, code named Operation Barbarossa, took the Soviet Union by surprise. Hitler began planning the attack when the Soviet Union expanded westward in the summer of 1940 and occupied Estonia, Latvia, Lithuania, and Romania. The Soviet Union had the largest intelligence network in the world, and yet Stalin refused to believe the countless warnings until hours before the Germans' first strike. Within a few days the front reached Maciejow.

Noike ran to main street when the German Army entered the town. They made a big show, parking their trucks less than a quarter mile outside of Maciejow, then parading down the street in their fine military gear—freshly pressed uniforms with elaborate belt buckles, black leather riding boots polished to a shine. Onlookers gawked at the men, unsure whether to admire or fear the impressive show of military force.

Ukrainian women from the neighboring villages arrived in traditional dress and offered flower garlands to the soldiers. The soldiers placed the garlands around their necks, smiling as they waved and thanked their supporters. Most Ukrainians simply wanted the Germans to improve their economic situation; others hoped their new occupiers would finally pave the way for an independent Ukrainian state, free of ethnic Russians, Poles, and Jews. Members of established Ukrainian nationalist groups were rumored to have made contact with the Germans weeks before Operation Barbarossa, taking steps to secure coveted government positions previously held by the Russians and their followers.

One of Maciejow's senior rabbis was also at the procession. He was an elderly man with a long, gray beard wearing a black hat and a *kapote*, a traditional black coat that brushed the ground. He had set up a small wooden table with bread and salt, the customary way to welcome visitors. The rabbi was extending his long, bony hand, offering a piece of bread and salt, when one soldier stepped out of the line, turned over the table, and shouted, "Get out of here!" Terrified, the rabbi hurried away, leaving his table and gifts behind.

*How could someone do this to a rabbi?*

Although the Soviets had transformed almost every aspect of life in Maciejow, they left the religious institutions and leaders alone. On Friday afternoons, the senior rabbi would put on his *kapote* and *streimel*, a round fur hat, and walk through the center of town, signaling the start of *Shabbat*, the Jewish Sabbath. One could hear the sound of store shutters closing as the rabbi passed through each block of town. The rabbis taught young and old, guiding the community for hundreds of years. Children would have to stand in the corner if they were disrespectful to them, yet this man had yelled at one of the most revered rabbis in the area.

When Noike shared the news with his mother later that afternoon, she tried to assure him that little had changed, but each day the world around him told a different story. One of the German authorities' first tasks was to post signs outlining the racial laws imposed in western Poland: Jews weren't allowed to walk on the sidewalk; Jews weren't allowed outside their homes between six in the evening and six in the morning; Jews were required to wear a white armband that was ten centimeters wide and embellished with a blue star of David.

Noike did not fully understand the significance of these laws until he saw a German soldier drag Pinie Broinstein, an elderly Jewish neighbor, off of the sidewalk. The soldier reprimanded him for walking on the sidewalk, pulled out his bayonet, and savagely hacked off his beard, cutting his skin with each stroke. Mr. Broinstein tried not to weep as blood oozed from his wounds and dripped onto his white shirt collar.

Noike wanted to protest the soldier's actions but he, too, was scared of the foreign giants with their guns and bayonets. He wondered if they would beat him if he walked on the sidewalk, or draw their guns if he was caught playing outside after curfew. Frightened, he again hurried home to tell his mother what he had witnessed.

"Noikele, look what Momma made for you today," she said, handing him a warm *pletzel* covered with poppy seeds, onions, and salt. She had been able to alleviate most of his fears with gentle words, but sometimes there was no way to explain why something had happened, no way to promise that it would not happen again. "Maybe you can bring one over to Mr. Broinstein to make him feel better."

Pesel urged Noike to stay close to home but he often wandered off, eager to investigate the latest commotion around town. He was walking over to the *Beis Medrush* synagogue, near the old market, when he saw a large fire burning in the center of the courtyard. One German soldier was ordering a bearded old man wearing morning prayer clothes—the *talles* shawl and *t'fillin*—to throw a Torah and other religious books into a fire, while two others were working a military camera: one ran the crank and the other filmed.

The old man held the books tightly, refusing to throw them into the fire.

The soldier started beating the old man with the butt of his rifle. The old man shook his head and quietly prayed as the rifle butt slammed into his back, his *yarmulka* slowly slipping from his head. The holy books eventually fell from his hands and were swallowed by the pyre. "Where is your God now?" one of the soldiers roared. "Where is your God now?" The film was made as propaganda to send back to Germany, to show that the work of the Third Reich was being carried out as planned.

The holy books were the same ones Noike had used in school. He started studying the Talmud and other scriptures even before he could walk. A man in the town, the *belfer*, would fetch children like Noike, carrying them on his shoulders to and from *cheder*, a home school for Judaic studies. They taught Noike to treat the holy books with respect. As he stood there watching the books burn, he was convinced that lightning would strike the soldiers down—that a God was watching—but nothing happened.

As a child who would strictly follow the rabbis and their teachings—sometimes too closely—Noike was bewildered by these incidents. A few years earlier his mother had served *Shabbat* soup without *mandlen*, Jewish soup nuts. "Where are the *mandlen*?" Noike demanded. "We don't have them today," his mother explained. "If there are no *mandlen*, there is no *Shabbat*," he said before blowing out the *Shabbat* candles. This story, which was retold many times over the years, made him infamous throughout their Jewish community.

It was after the book burning that the Germans forced the Jews to create a *Judenrat*, an administrative body of Jews who had to ensure that Nazi orders and regulations were implemented; *Judenrat* would eventually be established in Jewish communities throughout Europe. One of their first tasks was to round up Jews for daily work assignments. Women in Maciejow were often selected for gardening and cleaning tasks; men were typically selected for hard labor, or to make crafts that were useful to the Germans.

Pesel was assigned to weeding one of the vegetable gardens at German headquarters, which had been established in the former Catholic Monastery—the same place where the Red Army had been stationed. When she didn't return on time one afternoon, Noike decided to track her down.

"*Pan*, excuse me!" Noike called to a young guard standing near the vegetable gardens, smoking a cigarette. *Pan* was the customary way to address a man as "Sir"; women were addressed as *Pani*. "Where are the garden workers?"

"They went home for the day," he explained, tilting his head back as he blew a puff of smoke into the air.

"But my mother isn't home yet," Noike said.

"She might be inside the main building—they took some people for an additional assignment," the guard nodded towards headquarters.

Noike was friendly with the Polish gardener, known as an *ogrodnik*, who took care of the orchards next to German headquarters and lived in a small house on the property. The gardener sometimes asked Noike to deliver a basket of his best apples and plums to the Commandant. Noike would try to appear calm when he entered the Commandant's office; the vicious German Shepherd, who they called Ivan, was always at the Commandant's side. With an angry look, the Commandant would grab the basket and wave the little Jew away.

Noike took his usual route that afternoon, slipping through the back entrance and then heading towards the long staircase that led into the main building. Walking up the stairs he passed an older soldier who was on his way down.

"Where do you think you're going?" the soldier asked.

"My mother is working here—I want to find her," he explained.

"No, no—you can't go in there," the soldier snapped. "You go home now, young man, your mother will be home soon," he said, handing him a little harmonica.

The soldiers were humiliating the Jews inside, forcing the men onto all fours and then making the women ride them like horses. They took particular pleasure in harassing an overweight man, whipping him as he crawled on the floor. The Commandant unleashed his German Shepherd on this man and many others. All of these events were filmed with one of the hand-cranked cameras, entertainment for the people back in Germany. Decades after the war one of Noike's aunts told him about the film and how his mother had been forced to participate. His mother never mentioned what happened.

Later that summer, Noike was playing outside when he heard a crowd gathering in the main square. He recognized hundreds of his neighbors—men whom he used to see praying at the synagogue, shopping at the market, or strolling in the square—surrounded by SS and Gestapo (Nazi secret police) wielding machine guns. All of the Jewish males between the ages of sixteen and sixty had been ordered to turn in their Russian passports and get German ones. The men were forced to line up in rows of ten and marched off to German headquarters.

Noike saw the fear on their faces and ran home.

Years later a survivor told him what happened when they passed through the gate at the German headquarters. Both sides of their path were lined with Gestapo holding sticks the size of baseball bats. The men were pushed through and beaten severely; big German Shepherds gnawed at their heels, tearing their flesh. One of the Gestapo used his stick to start dividing the men into two groups: men who possessed certain craft skills—tailor, shoemaker, harness-maker, carpenter—were told to run home; the remaining four hundred were taken behind the headquarters and shot.

The Germans told the *Judenrat* that these men were sent to a labor camp and would return in one year. Within days, the families received letters from their loved ones, saying they were working hard and they would come home soon. The families did not have to examine the letters very closely to realize that someone other than their husband, father, uncle, or brother had written them. Noike also knew better: he saw the young Ukrainian laborers walking from headquarters with shovels; he heard the gunshots from his home.

    A tombstone now marks this place.

# 4

# SKULL AND CROSSBONES
*Maciejow, Poland. September 1941*

"*Aufmachen*, Yakob," the German soldiers shouted as they stood on the front stoop and banged their fists on the door. It was a cool night in late September, three months into the German occupation.

"Yakob" referred to Yakob Ginzburg, Noike's paternal grandfather, a deeply religious man who wore *peyos* (sidelocks) and attended synagogue twice a day. Noike's family had fled to his house when they saw the *Einsatzgruppen* motorcade enter town two days earlier. The *Einsatzgruppen*, a division of the SS, was a mobile death squad that came on motorcycles followed by trucks covered in thick, black canvas. Their last visit to Maciejow had been to kill the 400 young men and boys behind German headquarters.

News spread that the next *aktion*, as these roundups were called, would be less discriminating. Although the very old and those under sixteen years of age were still safe, women between sixteen and sixty were now vulnerable. Escaping from town was no longer an option, for the roads were heavily guarded and Jews were not permitted to own wagons, bicycles, or cars, or travel via public transportation. Maciejow's remaining Jews had no choice but to hide.

"*Aufmachen*, Yakob," the soldiers shouted again.

The soldiers began shining flashlights into Yakob's bedroom. Streams of light panned back and forth across the ceiling, searching for hidden trap doors. Noike recognized the soldiers' voices from earlier in the evening: young Ukrainian girls from across the street had been socializing with them and laughing at their jokes. Noike looked over at his brother Herschel, who was awake but too scared to move. Herschel was quite tall for his age and feared he would be mistaken for a boy of sixteen. Yakob was also awake but he was in poor health and unable to get out of bed. Noike realized that he was the only one who could speak on behalf of his family.

When Noike opened the door he saw two giant SS officers standing in front of the house; they glared down at the little boy in his pajamas. These men weren't ordinary SS officers, Noike realized: only the uniforms of senior officers were decorated in a confetti of badges, stripes, and medals. They wore the *Totenkopf* death squad mark—a skull and crossbones embossed in silver—on the front of their caps. The division was initially formed from concentration camp guards and men from an SS unit that fought the Polish Army back in 1939.

"Where are your sisters?" the first one barked in German.

Noike had never spoken to a German soldier, but the Germanic roots of the Yiddish language helped many Jews make the transition when necessary. "Sisters" implied the women of the household. Someone must have told the officers that his sister, mother, aunts, and grandmother had not been rounded up. The Germans relied on the locals to provide this information, offering money and extra rations—a few cigarettes, a liter of vodka, a kilo of sugar—in return.

"They took them away," Noike responded in Yiddish, acting as if he was on the verge of tears. "Mayb*e you* can tell me where they took them?" If he told the truth, they would all die; if he lied, he might save them all.

The soldiers pushed past him and entered the front room. Noike insisted that there were only three people in the house: his sick grandfather, his "younger" brother, and himself. Unconvinced, the soldiers began searching all of the rooms in the house, poking underneath beds and throwing open armoires but finding nothing.

"The basement—where is it?" the first soldier demanded, scanning for its entrance.

Noike led them to the cellar door located in the narrow hallway that connected the front room and the master bedroom. The first soldier pulled the door open; the second one drew his gun. Cool air rose from the cellar wall, sending a chill through Noike and making the little hairs on his arms and legs stand on end. The first soldier moved his flashlight's beam along the perimeter of the cellar walls, illuminating stores of butter, baskets of eggs, and sacks of potatoes. Nothing else was revealed.

"Show us the attic," the soldier demanded.

Noike pointed to the drop ladder in the hallway ceiling.

"Is anybody up there?" the soldier asked.

"No," Noike said, trying to hold the soldier's gaze.

The soldier pulled his pistol out of its holster and cocked the gun. He pointed it at the center of Noike's forehead and then pressed it firmly against his skin. The gun looked like a cannon to him; the long, cold, metal barrel was numbing.

"If somebody is up there, you're *kaput*," he warned him. "Are you sure nobody is up there?" he asked again.

"Yes, sir," Noike replied. "Nobody is up there."

The soldier with the flashlight pulled the attic door open, unfolded the ladder, and climbed up to search the attic.

Noike held his breath. His mother, sister, aunts, and grandmother were hiding in the second attic above the kitchen, which was accessible via a concealed trapdoor in the kitchen ceiling. The women had also taken steps to mask their age and beauty. Tears had streamed down Blima's face when her mother cut off her long, blonde hair a few days earlier. Pesel understood Blima's grief: as a teenager in Maciejow during the First World War, she was harassed by German soldiers when she walked through town. She never imagined that her daughter would have the same experience; she never imagined that she would find herself, at the age of thirty-six, covering her hair in a *babushka* and impersonating an old woman.

"Did you find somebody?" The soldier, still pressing his gun against Noike's forehead, called up to the attic with impatience.

"*Nisht*," the other replied, climbing back down the ladder.

The two soldiers conversed in rapid German, too fast for Noike to understand, then barked their next order: "Take us to the garden." The Ukrainian girls must have given the soldiers some clues since few homes had gardens large enough to provide cover for one person, let alone five. Although the gun had been pulled away from from Noike's forehead, he could still feel the cold metal.

Noike led them to the back door that opened onto the garden. Walking through the house he thought of his family—his "sisters"—crouched above them. If someone coughed, sneezed, or shifted, the officers would hear them and it would be over for everyone. The soldiers walked into the vast garden, which was brimming over with lettuce, tomatoes, potatoes, and even tobacco. Noike shut the door behind them as it started to rain.

Noike pressed his ear against the door and listened as the soldiers weaved through the rows of vegetables, stomping on the lettuce and other vegetables in their path. After a brief silence he heard them leave the garden, walk along the side of the house, then head towards the street in the front of the house, off to raid another Jewish family. Their footsteps grew quieter; then at last there was silence.

Although he could breathe again, Noike's teeth were chattering like a machine gun. Herschel helped him back into bed and held him until he fell asleep.

ABOUT A WEEK LATER WORD SPREAD THAT THE RAIDS were officially over and the *Einsatzgruppen* had moved on to another town. The *aktion* had been a success from the German perspective: 1,500 Jews had been killed—a full third of the local Jewish population. Those who survived the raids emerged from their hiding places in cellars, barns, attics, fields, and the woods. They found the streets scattered with bits and pieces of fabric, torn from their family, friends, and neighbors as they tried to escape from their attackers.

When Noike and his family returned home, a longtime neighbor was waiting near the front door with a small bundle. Pesel looked down at the bundle and immediately understood: it was the crocheted shawl that had belonged to her mother, Beila, who had worn it nearly every day.

Beila had refused to leave the house when the rest of the family went into hiding; she had grown senile in recent years and would not listen to reason. "Nobody is going to force me to run from my home," she had said repeatedly, shaking her head. Her shawl was found near the sidewalk, amid the other personal effects that littered the street, their owners long gone. Beila had raised her family in that house; she was the first one killed.

Noike had never experienced the death of someone close to him, let alone lost someone in such a brutal fashion. He could not comprehend why the Germans would kill someone as harmless as his grandmother. He imagined the Germans dragging her away and wished he could have been there to protect her, as he did his "sisters." He pictured himself standing in the doorway, steadfastly convincing the soldiers that no one was in the house except for him.

Pesel changed into black clothing and covered the mirrors according to Jewish tradition. She gathered her children to say the mourner's *kaddish*, a prayer honoring the dead, and thought of her mother's good deeds, praying that no one else would meet the same fate. *Kaddishes* were being said all over town; most women no longer had sons, husbands, or uncles. Hundreds of women had also been murdered, leaving many small children wandering the streets and nearby fields without parents. The *Judenrat* collected furniture and other household items from the abandoned houses and created an orphanage. Adult survivors took turns helping to feed, bathe, and comfort the little ones.

WINTER CAME AND LIFE WENT BACK TO NORMAL, although to the Jews of Maciejow, "normal" became a relative term. One afternoon soon after the first snow, Noike was heading to a neighbor's house when he noticed an old *rebbe*, a teacher of Hebrew and the Bible, walking on the edge of the road. A group of German soldiers pulled up in a horse-drawn sleigh, the customary way to travel in winter. One soldier dismounted the sleigh and pushed the old man into the snow, causing his hat to tumble to the ground. Then the soldier made him pick it up, fill it with snow, and put it back on his head. All of the soldiers laughed as the snow dripped down his face, into his shirt collar. After taunting him a little more, the soldier got back on the sled and they drove away.

Many ethnic Ukrainians were quick to take full advantage of their neighbors' weakened positions. For years Herschel had begged his mother for skis. Knowing she could not afford them, he started putting aside his own money and somehow managed to save enough to buy them that winter. The skis were made of cheap wood and fitted with leather ankle straps; no special shoes were required. On one of his first outings, a ski trip with friends, he returned home empty-handed.

"Where are your skis?" Noike asked, trailing Hershel as he stormed off to their bedroom. He had hoped Herschel might loan them to him one day.

"Now Jews can't have skis!" Herschel fumed as he paced the room.

He had been skiing with a group of Jewish boys on the outskirts of town when a couple of Ukrainian farm boys came upon them. "Jews aren't allowed to own skis," one of the boys had said. "Give them to us or we'll call the

Gestapo," another leered, knowing the Gestapo would punish even young Jews for the smallest violations.

Noike felt sorry for his brother; Herschel had wanted those skis so badly.

Later that winter German soldiers came to their house, this time demanding that his mother hand over all of her fur coats. Their countrymen were fighting in the harsh Russian winter and freezing to death; trains filled with wounded and frostbitten German soldiers had been passing through Maciejow in recent weeks. Noike watched with anger as his mother went to the hallway closet and returned with a dusty box containing her late husband's fur coats; she had kept all of them. She kept almost all of his things for years after he died, until the Germans came and started taking everything away.

# 5

# HAVING SECOND THOUGHTS
*Florida, February 2006*

A few days into my Florida visit, I woke to an unusually quiet house. I assumed that my parents were immersed in the morning newspaper but no one was in the kitchen. Eager to make the most of my time with my father, I started setting up the video camera and reviewing the questions I had prepared the night before.

"I don't know why, but I didn't sleep well last night," my father said as he walked into the kitchen. "I think I'm going to lie down for a few minutes."

"All right, well, I was hoping we could get started on '42 but we don't have to do it today. We covered a lot of material over the last few days—1939, 1940, 1941," I said, starting to wonder if I had gone too fast, if the interviews had taken a toll.

He went into his office and closed the door.

Aside from the "little boy" stories, my father rarely spoke to anyone about his wartime experiences. He started to open up around the fiftieth anniversary of the end of the war, when he learned about an international conference for children who had spent the Holocaust in hiding. The organizers had expected a few hundred attendees but almost two thousand people gathered together and broke their silence. Around the same time, many educators, reporters, and filmmakers were reaching out to survivors, wanting to document their stories for future generations. My father was reluctant at first but soon agreed to a number of private interviews and eventually public talks.

Our interviews would be different, I soon learned.

He shaped most of the agenda that first day, providing me with background on his town and summarizing relevant historical events. But in the days that followed, I started to probe, hoping to lead him down new paths. While he was recounting about the story of hiding at his paternal grandfather's house I realized that I was missing a piece of information: "Was your maternal grandmother hiding in another house?" I asked.

"I never told anyone this, but…" he glanced at me and then at the floor, thinking back. Suddenly he brought his hands up to cover his face.

I stood up to try and comfort him but he remained stiff, his arms pressed close to his body. He had always been a slight man but he suddenly looked frail, fragile, somehow more human. "Should we stop?" I asked. My hands shook as I reached to turn off the video camera.

"No, I want to continue," he said. Then he described the details of her death: the stubbornness, the raids, the shawl found in the street.

The writer in me felt that I had made a breakthrough; the daughter in me felt tremendous guilt. Was my quest for knowledge at the expense of his suffering? I did not want to cause him pain, or force him to relive the most tragic moments of his life, but it did not seem possible to avoid it. And this was just the beginning of the war. Would *I* even be able to keep it together when the story got even worse? I, too, had not slept well the previous night, thinking about how I had upset my father. But a sense of responsibility urged me to continue.

When he resurfaced that afternoon I suggested that we spend the rest of the day relaxing at the community pool, a short drive from the house. Taking a break and slowing things down seemed like the only choice. As I read my book I looked over at my father, who was sleeping peacefully as the sun beat down on his face, his arms, his legs. He wasn't wearing any sunglasses or sunblock; he had refused to let anything get between him and the sun over the years.

"You know, we don't have to write the book," I said when he woke up. Although I was committed to pressing ahead, I felt I should give him an out.

"No, I'm fine," he insisted. "I was just feeling tired today."

"Well, you can change your mind anytime," I said, still worried about him.

Back in San Francisco a few days later I reviewed our interviews, as well as the essays my father wrote in a writing workshop for Holocaust survivors. Piecing the old and new together, I started emailing him rough drafts. Initially they resembled a book of MadLibs: the pages were dotted with empty spaces for details on people, places, and events. Writing the stories, I thought, might be easier than face-to-face interviews, easier for both of us. Maybe looking at me—the daughter named after one of his loved ones—

forced him to acknowledge what had happened in a way he had never allowed himself.

Eager to fully immerse myself in the project, I started renting Holocaust documentaries. The films would sit on my dining table for one week, then another. After writing about the Holocaust all day, I dreaded watching the videos at night; it was too painful to be confronted with real, live voices detailing events similar to the ones playing over and over in my head. Eventually I would send the videos back and rent comedies and love stories instead.

I bought pink tulips for my apartment; I started taking yoga.

Lying on my back in the *savasana* yoga pose (the "corpse" pose) our instructor gently urged the class to free our minds of all thoughts from the day, to focus on our breathing. As I tried to clear my mind, I found myself drawn to the very images I was trying to forget for those five minutes: the *rebbe* reaching his long, bony hand out to the German soldier; the old man forced to burn the holy books; my great grandmother being taken away by the SS. My instructor's voice roused me from the morbid pose: "Open your eyes and turn to your right side."

A few weeks after my return from Florida I started finding large envelopes crammed into my mailbox, sent by my father via U.S. Priority Mail. The first package contained photos of his town, a sketch depicting one of his escape routes, and stories about life before the war. "*Rosh Hashanah*, the Jewish New Year, was one of the most festive days for the Jews of Maciejow," my father wrote. "Weeks before the holiday, my mother would take us to the tailor to get fitted for our new clothes: tweed suits for my brother and I, a printed dress for my sister." When the holiday finally arrived, his family would attend synagogue together and wish for *gezunt* and *parnusse*, health and good fortune. My father would race home after the services, eager to read the holiday cards delivered by the postman and taste his favorite holiday foods—*gelfite* fish and chicken soup. All of these traditions came to an end under the German occupation.

# 6

## THE BASEMENT
*Maciejow Poland. September 1942*

The town synagogues were still shuttered when *Rosh Hashanah* arrived the following September, but most Jews continued to pray in secret, inside their homes. Noike and his brother were invited to one of these clandestine gatherings, this one held at a neighbor's house down the road. They quietly entered through the back door, closely guarded by two teenaged boys from their school. "*Shana Tova*," the young guards whispered as they ushered the boys into the house.

At least thirty worshippers were crammed into the tiny living room. They leaned against archways, squatted on the floor, and sat on the occasional chair. In the center of the room a group of older men wearing prayer shawls were huddled around the Torah, swaying from side to side as they sang. The prayers were the same ones they read every year but the atmosphere had never been so tense. Posters all over town had warned Jews about large gatherings: "More than three Jews found in assembly are to be shot instantly." But forgoing prayer was not an option for these religious Jews: *Rosh Hashanah* was judgment day, the time when God would decide who should live and who should die.

One of the men leading the prayers, Itzchak Shochat, was dressed in a *kittel*, a white robe worn on religious occasions such as this one. Itzchak had a beautiful, long white beard, soft as cotton. He belonged to the same synagogue as Noike's family, the Trysker Synagogue, and sat in the same section as Noike's grandfather. "Noikele, come here," Itzchak would say after the *Shabbat* services, "such a *sheina punem*." Squatting down, he would reach out and pinch Noike's cheeks until they turned pink. It hurt but Noike liked his attention.

As they were softly chanting the holiday prayers, one of the boys on watch ran into the living room and announced that two SS officers were heading towards the house. Itzchak grabbed the Torah, stuffed it underneath his *kittel*, and ran out the back door. The worshippers frantically hid their prayer clothes and books, placing them behind curtains, inside furniture, under couch cushions. Noike stuffed his prayer book inside his coat.

Within seconds two SS officers stormed into the living room with their guns drawn. They wore riding pants, black leather boots, and tall hats with the *Totenkopf* symbol, the skull and crossbones, the same uniform worn by officers who had raided Noike's grandfather's house the previous summer.

"Jewish assemblies are forbidden!" one officer shouted in German; the other panned his gun across the room.

The worshippers remained silent.

"Raus, raus!" he ordered the group. "Everyone must leave immediately!"

Noike kept his head bowed as he followed his neighbors out of the house.

No one was arrested that day; no one was instantly shot. Hours later the reason for the reprieve became clear: a large-scale massacre, an *aktion*, was planned for Monday. One leak came from a Jewish woman, Sheva Berelson, who worked as a maid at German headquarters and had befriended a soldier in recent months. Upon learning that Jewish workers would not be needed that Monday, she asked her soldier friend about the sudden change in schedule. He confided that the situation would get much worse for the Jews in Maciejow—pregnant women would soon be removed from the Jewish clinics and shot.

Another leak came from a Ukrainian hospital administrator who was close friends with Avram Avruch, a Jewish doctor who studied medicine in Switzerland and was fluent in German. Avram was no longer allowed to treat non-Jewish patients—a racial law introduced by the Germans—but he wrote medical reports and completed other hospital administrative tasks that had to be done in German. The hospital administrator told Avram that the next *aktion* would be the final one.

Noike's mother, Pesel, tried to maintain a sense of calm around her children, even as she prepared for the inevitable. She went from house to house, meeting with close friends and relatives; they exchanged what little information they had on the raids and their strategies for survival. After everything had been arranged, Pesel shared her plans with her children: "We are going to stay with Gitel Silverberg for a few days. She has built a hiding place in her basement and will let us stay there until the next *aktion* is over. The *rebbe* also has a secret room, but it's too small for all of us."

Hiding places had saved many people during the last *aktion*; this plan seemed to be their only hope. Gitel Silverberg, a second cousin, started building her hiding place a few months earlier, a short time after a Polish woman returned from the neighboring town of Kovel and told her Jewish friends about corpses lying in the streets. The Germans had massacred 15,000 Jews, decimating Kovel's entire Jewish population.

"But what about all of our things?" Noike's sister Blima asked.

Many homes had been ransacked during the raids of the previous summer. The police had been the biggest culprits but many peasants from the neighboring villages had also plundered. Anything left out in the open was for the taking: dishes, armoires, mattresses, bed frames, clothing—even children's toys.

"We can bring some blankets and food," Pesel said. "But the police will be suspicious if they see us leaving the house with anything else. We'll hide the silver and photographs later tonight." One room was left unfinished when Pesel expanded their home before the war; she planned to bury the silver, photographs, and other family heirlooms under its bare, clay floor.

The next afternoon the four of them left their home, keeping everything but their most sentimental valuables in place. They locked the door and crossed town as if they were on an ordinary social call, visiting neighbors for afternoon tea. But instead of walking as one group, they split into two: Noike and his mother walked through one side of the square; Herschel and Blima walked through the other. Noike followed his mother, clutching at his pillow.

They entered the hiding place through an outhouse behind Gitel Silverberg's grocery store. Pesel and Herschel went inside first, pushing the toilet aside to reveal a tiny dirt entrance carved into the floor. One by one they squeezed through the hole and climbed down a long, narrow ladder. At the base of the ladder was a short passageway that led into a room.

The basement was crowded with at least fifty people, mostly women with young children, the only demographics left in Maciejow. It was dark but in one corner Noike could make out Gitel Silverberg's lively brown eyes and warm smile. She was wearing a long, black dress and had a *babushka* over her hair like his mother. He also saw his brother's friend Haim Rosenberg sitting with his mother and sister.

Pesel led them through the basement until she found an open spot away from the original entrance. Gitel had sealed off and painted the door when they created the hiding place but one could still see the street through small cracks along the bottom. Pesel laid a blanket across the cool cement floor, trying to secure enough room for her family to sleep later that night. Noike sat down with his mother while Herschel and Blima wandered off to another corner and searched for friends.

There was little to do in the basement: moving around too much would create noise; talking too much would create noise. Most people huddled in small groups, whispering to each other, eventually nodding off in the darkness as nighttime approached. Pesel started humming as she stroked Noike's back. As a young girl she sang with the local Yiddish theater group; it was there that she met her husband Kalman, a talented violinist and actor who died less than two years after Noike was born. She stopped performing many years ago but she still sang around her family. That evening, she sang a familiar lullaby to young Noike:

> *Pretty like the moon*
> *Bright like the stars*
> *From Heaven you were*
> *Sent to me as a present.*

Noike leaned against his mother and imagined lying in his bed at home, nestled under a thick layer of goose down bedding. Soothed by the lullaby, he was starting to fall asleep when he heard Blima talking to his mother.

"We're going to hide in the Pearlman's attic for the rest of the night," Blima whispered, motioning to a group of teenagers gathering near the entrance to the hiding place. "We'll head to the woods before sunrise—some of the boys have built a bunker." Many of the teenagers who had escaped to the woods during the previous raids had managed to survive. In the forests they could occasionally breathe fresh air and would have somewhere to run if discovered.

"Blimele, I don't think it's such a good idea," Pesel said, shaking her head. "We should all stay together."

Pesel eventually resigned herself to Blima's decision. Children were no longer children in those days; the fight for survival forced them to think and act like adults. Noike reached his arms out to embrace his sister. She bent down and placed a kiss on his forehead as he hugged her legs, which were covered in layers of wool stockings and long underwear. He watched intently as she crossed the room then disappeared down the passageway.

Gunshots shattered the early morning silence. Some people in the basement had been sleeping but most had stayed awake all night, unable to rest knowing that the *aktion* was imminent. Women grabbed their children and hurried into the darkest corners of the basement, barricading themselves behind boxes and wooden crates. Herschel and the other teenage boys ran towards the original entrance, taking turns to peek through the cracks and provide updates for the group. "They shot Esther!" one of the boys announced.

Esther and her elderly mother owned a small corner store that sold candy, ice cream, and soda; her father was killed in one of the earlier *aktions*. When the police had tried to drag Esther's mother out of their home that morning Esther stood in their way, hysterically crying and begging the officers to leave them alone. The police ordered Esther to step aside and quiet down. As she fell to her knees one of them pulled out his gun and shot Esther, right in front of her mother.

The Germans had assembled the police force a short time after the occupation. Young men were typically recruited from neighboring farming villages with large Ukrainian nationalist populations and trained by the SS. Many of them had criminal records and had done time in Polish prisons; others were poor peasants desperate for work. Because the force was composed of ethnic Ukrainians and backed by Ukrainian leaders, they were often referred to as the "Ukrainian police." At first they helped enforce the curfew, later on they passed out the armbands; in the end they dragged women and children from their homes.

Ukrainian police continued to go house to house, pushing people out into the street and then taking them to the big synagogue, *Beis Medrush*, where they were forced to line up and kneel on the cobblestones as the German officers collected their valuables. After they had captured about seventy-five people, they would march them from *Beis Medrush* to the lime mines on the edge of town. As the Jews approached the mines they immediately understood their fate. *Einsatzgruppen* shooters were standing behind bushes near the mass grave, which was filled with the victims that came before them. The Jews were forced to stand in front of the grave and undress as they heard their neighbors slowly dying in the earth below. Some would try to escape, others would yell obscenities at their murderers; most would kiss their loved ones goodbye and pray for a quick death. The murderers left the graves uncovered until their work was done, almost two weeks later.

Decades after the war, Noike met a teenage boy who had survived the graves: Rubin Grosser. Rubin thought he was dead when the bullet struck his head, but the wound was superficial. He remained motionless in the grave as they continued to shoot his family, friends, and neighbors. When the *Einsatzgruppen* left the site that evening he started to crawl out of the grave, pushing through the mountain of dead bodies. He was about to run off when he heard moans coming from a boy beside him, Leibel Naimark. Naked and bloody, the two of them ran to a farmer who had offered to help when word first spread of the *aktion*. The farmer and his wife nursed the boys back to health and sheltered them until it was safe to leave. Rubin and Leibel were among the very few to survive the graves; the earth was said to be shaking for four weeks.

Everyone in Gitel's basement remained silent as the raids continued, except for one little girl who couldn't stop crying. Each time she wailed, the others in the basement would look towards the mother. "Please do something," their eyes begged. The others were sympathetic—many were mothers themselves—but they also feared for their own lives. When the girl finally settled down and fell asleep, the mother slipped out of the basement and put her in the house next door.

At some point the little girl woke up, or the Ukrainian police came into the house and woke her up; no one knows exactly how it happened. The police brought her outside and asked: "Where's your mother?" She immediately ran to the outhouse and wept, "Momma, Momma." The police opened the outhouse door and checked inside, but found nothing.

The police started to walk away but the little girl refused to move. Clinging to the edge of the outhouse door she continued to cry: "Momma, Momma." The police went back to the outhouse, poked around the seat, and then finally nudged the toilet aside, revealing the entrance to the hiding place. One of them stuck his rifle inside the hole and yelled in Ukrainian: "*Vilezai!* Come out!"

With no place to run, the women and children started filing out of the basement. Noike and his mother were on the far side of the room, a safe distance from the police who continued to shout, "*Vilezai, Vilezai!*" Pesel scanned the room for Herschel but it was difficult to see in the darkness, or to shout over the weeping women and children. They had stood to follow the others when Pesel noticed a section of wall that was loosely boarded.

"Noikele, quick, get inside," she said, pulling a board off the wall.

He crawled inside and stepped as far back as he could.

"Hold this in place and don't move until it's safe," she instructed him, handing him the board with the nails pointed in his direction.

Noike grabbed the nails, held them tightly, not moving a limb.

Pesel hid under some bedding; everyone else had left by now.

Through the cracks in the wood, Noike saw three Ukrainian police wearing their signature black uniforms with the word *Militzia* printed on the back enter the hiding place and begin looking for valuables and any remaining Jews. As two of them hunted for valuables, a third walked around the room, thrusting his bayonet into possible hiding places. Every few minutes a match would strike, illuminating the darkest corners of the basement. In the faint light Noike saw the officer with the bayonet, a young man not more than twenty, approach the place where his mother was hiding. The man raised the bayonet over his shoulder and sank it into the pile of bedding. "No, no," Pesel cried, pierced by the bayonet, "I'm coming out!"

Noike froze; he was afraid to breathe.

He watched the police officer grab his mother by the arm and lead her out of the hiding place. He wanted to do something—to shout, to attack, to run—but his mouth, arms, and legs obeyed his mother's last words: *Don't move until it's safe. Don't move until it's safe. Don't move until it's safe.* Her figure grew smaller and smaller as they neared the outhouse entrance.

And then she was gone.

The two other officers continued to search the basement, kicking over empty boxes and crates, opening any packages left behind. One of the men stopped a few inches away from Noike and paused to light a cigarette. He was so close that Noike could smell the phosphorous from the match, the first puff of cigarette smoke. The man slid the matchbook back inside his pocket and walked away.

When they finally left Noike slowly let out his breath.

He remained frozen with fear behind the wall, listening for sounds of the police. Sometime later another man came down into the hiding place wearing a dark, threadbare suit. Noike stood still, unsure whether it was safe to come out. As he squinted through the cracks in the wood he recognized the man as Moishe Burshtein, the head of the *Judenrat*. He had been a community leader before the war, organizing fundraisers for the poor and celebrations during the Jewish holidays. The German authorities forced him into the *Judenrat* role, threatening him and his family with death if he did not cooperate. With the raids almost complete, they no longer had any use for him.

Noike stepped away from the wall and slowly walked over to Mr. Burshtein. "I'm looking for galoshes," Mr. Burshtein said, his forehead damp with sweat. "I'm going to the woods tonight—it's muddy there." He seemed disoriented, as if he had just awoken from a deep sleep. Noike was also in a dream-like state, his mind and body following a script unknown to him. The hiding place, the police with the bayonet, his mother's capture—none of it seemed real.

"Moishe, where are you going now?" Noike grabbed at the man's sleeve. He had no plan, nowhere to go.

"Next door," Mr. Burshtein said, nodding towards the other house. "They might have some galoshes in the attic."

Noike followed him into the open-air attic, which was littered with bits and pieces of old furniture. They were moving an old trunk when they heard a noise near the foot of the ladder. Mr. Burshtein glanced down, meeting the eyes of a Ukrainian police officer who was pointing a rifle directly at him.

"Get down here!" the policeman ordered. "Is anyone else up there?"

"Nobody, just me," Mr. Burshtein's voice quivered.

Unsatisfied, the policeman called over another officer to guard Mr. Burshtein while he searched the attic.

Noike crawled into the far corner of the attic, into the small space where the slant of the roof met the floor. Terrified of capture, he pressed his body against the attic wall, disappearing into its dark shadows. As he lay there, he heard the policeman climbing the ladder, a brief pause, then the sound of his descent.

"The Jew was telling the truth," he said to the other officer. They hauled Mr. Burshtein off to the synagogue, never to be seen again.

Noike knew the attic would not be safe for very long. He remembered another hiding place his mother had mentioned: the *rebbe*'s house, only a few doors down. *The rebbe*'s daughter, Malka, owned a popular ready-to-wear clothing store.

Noike descended the ladder and looked down the street. He was met by a religious silence: all of the homes had been Jewish; all of them had been raided. Pressing his body against the white picket fence, he sidled past one, two, three houses, until he reached the *rebbe*'s house. He walked inside and surveyed the main room: it had already been ransacked by the locals so most of the furniture was missing; unwanted items were discarded on the floor.

"Malka," he began to call quietly, "Malka."

No answer.

Again, he called, "Malka, Malka."

No answer.

He started to leave the house when he heard someone say, "Shhh…"

He turned around and saw a board raised in the wall, under a table in the corner of the room. As he neared the opening, two hands reached out and dragged him inside.

He fainted.

# 7

# THE LITTLE SEPIA PHOTO
*New York, circa 1980*

The wooden dresser in my parents' bedroom was too tall for me to reach when I was little, but I could see it from a distance, reach it if I pulled over a chair. Sometimes I carried over the vanity chair from the master bathroom, other times I dragged the wicker chair from beside the television. Eventually I could stand on my tiptoes, stretch my arms out, and run my fingers across the shiny, lacquered surface. On it rested a ceramic vase from China, a wooden jewelry box from Japan, and framed photos of my grandparents.

My hands would immediately gravitate to the framed pictures.

The large, color photo of my maternal grandparents was taken at my parents' wedding reception, in front of a blue, floral background. My maternal grandmother, whom I called *Baba*, is in a pink, satiny dress and has her dark, brown hair pulled into a tight bun. Her arm is wrapped around my grandfather, who is dressed in a black tuxedo. He has jet-black hair and a pencil-thin mustache; both are neatly trimmed. I never knew this grandfather but my *Baba* often referred to him as my *Zeidi* and said that he was a "good man." A few months before she died, she told me she would be seeing him soon.

The photo of my paternal grandparents was much smaller in size and more mysterious: their image is painted in sepia tones; they are floating in front of a solid sepia background. The photo must have been taken somewhere in Europe, I guessed. My grandmother looks very fashionable in the photo, her hair done in the finger wave style I had seen in old movies. My grandfather is wearing a tweed, three-piece suit with a skinny tie and a handkerchief in one pocket.

I first understood that they were dead when I learned that my siblings were named after them: my sister after Pesel, my brother after Kalman. My mother told me that my Grandfather Kalman died *before* the war, while my Grandmother Pesel died *during* the war. I somehow understood that *during* the war implied a more tragic end; I never dared to ask for more detail. They were never referred to as my *Baba* or my *Zeidi*; their premature deaths somehow robbed them of our familial endearments.

When no one was looking I would take the frames down from the dresser and gently place them in an arc on the nubby yellow carpet, as if they were guests at a tea party. Sitting cross-legged on the floor, I would pick up the picture of my paternal grandparents by the edges of its lacy gold frame, careful not to get my fingerprints on the glass. The little photo was magical, a secret portal to my lost grandparents. Did I have his eyes? Her smile? I would stare into the photograph, trying to venture back in time, wondering what it would be like to meet them.

I would close my eyes and picture myself in their living room.

"I've heard so much about you *Suzala*," I imagined my Grandmother Pesel saying. All of the older relatives liked to call me *Suzala*; I imagined she would do the same. "Would you like some *fluden*?" she tilted her head as she asked. "I just took it out of the oven."

I nodded my head, eager to try the sweet-smelling pastry.

"Save some *fluden* for me," my Grandfather Kalman chuckled as he entered the room. "Shall I play some violin for you, *mamela*? I hear you've been taking lessons at school." My grandfather grinned, somehow sensing that I had been having difficulty.

"Yes, my friend Heidi and I take lessons together," I replied eagerly. "But we can't stand our teacher, Mr. Van Houten—he makes us practice the same boring piece over and over."

We would continue to talk about all of the things that I thought grandchildren and grandparents should know about each other—birthdays, favorite colors, favorite desserts—until I heard someone coming up the stairs. They would nod their heads, letting me know it was all right to say goodbye. As I kissed them through the glass frames, I would tell them that I loved them and promise to visit again soon. Standing on my tiptoes, I would reach forward, carefully placing the photos back on top of the dresser, positioning them exactly as I found them.

# 8

# MALKA'S HOUSE
*Maciejow, Poland. September 1942*

Someone in the *rebbe*'s house gave Noike a swig of whiskey to revive him. He never imagined that his first taste of the grown-up drink would come so soon—at the age of eleven—in a dark room with neighbors he had only seen in passing at the synagogue. The only alcohol he had tried before that time was the holy wine served on holidays and *Shabbat*.

He wiped his mouth with the back of his hand, sat up, and surveyed his surroundings: two narrow rooms connected through an open doorway. The rooms had been used as bedrooms until the entrance was boarded up and painted, making it seem like the end of the house. Each room had a small window covered in thick, dark cloth. The space was dim during the day, pitch black at night.

"You're awake," a voice whispered. Noike looked up at Yosi Mach, a young man of twenty who had lived across the street from Malka's house. Srulek Silverberg, Gitel Silverberg's teenaged son, was also sitting nearby. The *rebbe*, his wife, and their two grown children, Malka and Mendel, were huddled in the other room. Everyone was sparsely dressed; the small space had grown uncomfortably close—warmer with each new arrival.

"They took them all away," Noike said, looking at the boys.

"We know," Srulek said, his dark brown eyes downcast. "We heard them marching to the synagogue."

Srulek and Yosi had managed to survive the raids but had been separated from their respective parents, brothers, and sisters in the chaos. They, too, remembered that the *rebbe* had a small hiding place and ran there during the raids. All three of them had lost loved ones but no one could mourn; they still feared for their own lives. Instead, they fell into the rhythms and rules the *rebbe* and his family had established in the hiding place.

When the water barrel needed to be replenished, the boys would slip out to the neighborhood well, footsteps away from the entrance to Malka's house. Yosi and Srulek would attach the bucket to the chain, lower it down, then crank it back up, careful to make as little noise as possible. Noike would stand on the road to the post office, keeping watch in case the night patrol approached. Yosi, being the oldest boy, would venture out for food in the middle of the night. He usually went to the other side of town, where a long-time Ukrainian friend would give him a loaf of bread. When he returned with the bread, Malka's mother would divide it between the seven of them, one fistful per person each day.

One morning Malka's mother announced that they would not get any bread that day, for it was *Yom Kippur*, the Jewish day of atonement, which was traditionally observed with a one-day fast. She was determined to follow Jewish traditions and laws, no matter the circumstances; she even continued to wear her *shaitel*, a wig worn by married Orthodox Jewish women. She also handed the boys *mahzorim*, prayer books used on the High Holidays of *Rosh Hashanah* and *Yom Kippur*.

Noike opened his *mahzor* to the *Yom Kippur* prayers but his lips wouldn't move, the words would not come out. As he stared at the pages, he could hear shots coming from the lime mines, where they continued to kill Jews captured in the raids. He thought of his mother, brother, and sister and envisioned their last moments at the lime mines. *Where was God then? Why did God let innocent people die?* This would be the first time in his young life that he questioned the words of the rabbis, questioned his religion—questioned his God.

The first Saturday night after Noike joined the hiding place, Yosi left to get food and failed to return within the usual time frame. They hoped he was staying in another part of town for the night, that he would return at daybreak, but he never came back. They weren't only concerned about his well-being: Yosi had been their sole source of food.

"I'll get some fruit," Noike volunteered the next morning. He wanted to go to the orchard behind German headquarters, where he knew the Polish gardener—the *ogrodnik*—and his family.

"Noike, you can't go out during the day," Malka said, shaking her head. "The police are still patrolling—someone will spot you the minute you reach the main street." She was in her late twenties but had seemed to age more than a decade over the past week: streaks of gray lined her short, black hair; dark circles framed her hazel eyes.

"Do you have any small farming outfits?" Noike asked.

He wanted to disguise himself as a young Ukrainian farm boy, to blend in with the people heading to church that Sunday. He recalled seeing farming clothes in Malka's ready-to-wear store.

"Yes, I may have something that would fit you," Malka said. She walked over to the dresser in the other room and sifted through one of the drawers. "Try these," she said, handing him a pile of black shirts and pants in various sizes.

The first set was too big: the shirt billowed out like a potato sack and the pants fell to the ground, surrounding him in a puddle of black. The other set, still too large, would have to do. He rolled up the sleeves, folded over the elastic waist, and waited for the sound of church bells.

Around noon the bells started ringing as expected: *ding ding* went the Polish ones; *gong gong* went the Ukrainian ones. He stuffed a small knife they had given him into his pocket and squeezed out of the hiding place, passing through the same small entrance in the corner of the living room.

"Be careful, Noike," Malka said as she closed up the entrance.

The main street was quieter than he had expected; everyone had already left for church. He continued walking towards the orchards, passing the homes of his Jewish neighbors, murdered less than one week ago: the Rosenbergs, the Schneiders, the Broinshteins, the Kalatzkis, the Schwartzes. When he reached his street, he glanced towards his house, the second one on the left. The bedroom window was open, his mother's silk curtains blowing in the wind. For just a moment, he imagined coming home from school, the silk curtains a cue that she was waiting for him. He would enter the house and find her standing over the stove, preparing the evening meal.

"What did you learn at school today?" Pesel would ask, leaning over to give him a bite of the egg noodles, the boiled potatoes, the beef brisket.

He thought back to the time, not long ago, when he handed her his report card with the Russian word *vidminnik* printed on it. He didn't know what the words meant but she did: "Noikele, my little boy, the teacher says you did an outstanding job!" she said to him, stroking his head.

He was gazing at the silk curtains and thinking of his mother when a young girl's voice suddenly asked in Polish: "Noika, where are you going?" He looked over and saw his neighbor's daughter, Anna, standing on the corner in her Sunday best, a freshly pressed pinafore and embroidered cotton blouse. She was about the same age as Noike.

"That old Russian woman and her grandson moved into your house," Anna said as she stepped towards Noike. She was referring to the woman who would light their stove on the Sabbath, for Jewish law prohibited such "work" from sundown on Friday until nightfall on Saturday. The woman used to struggle to rent one room in a Jewish home across the street; now she had a furnished house all to herself.

"Sorry, Anna, I have to go meet someone," Noike said, hurrying away from the girl. Anna seemed to mean no harm but he worried she would tell others about him, especially the old Russian woman who must have thought his entire family was dead. She would not be pleased to discover that one had survived.

Noike reached the orchard and found Elizabeta, the gardener's wife, sitting outside alone, waiting for her husband and daughter to return from church services. She was wearing a brightly colored dress and a white kerchief to protect her from the afternoon sun. Elizabeta gasped and crossed herself when she saw Noike walking up the pathway.

*How could this boy be alive? All of the Jews in Maciejow are dead.*

Noike was alive but he was not the same happy boy she had known. He had a grave expression on his face, the kind of expression reserved for adults in mourning. He was unnaturally pale and the ill-fitting farm clothes made him appear thinner than she remembered.

"Noika, come inside, someone might see you," she said in Polish, ushering him into the house and closing the door.

"They took everyone away," he told her. "Have you seen my mother?" Noike asked, hoping his mother might have been able to escape from the police.

"No, dear, I have not," she said, gently placing her hand on his shoulder. Elizabeta had known his family for many years, and remembered when each child had been born. "You should stay in our attic until the orchard workers leave for the day." The workers were mostly young Ukrainian men from the villages, many eager to collect the reward for turning in Jews.

Elizabeta led him to the attic and passed him apples, pears, and a chunk of bread—the most food he had seen in over a week. Noike thanked her as she shut the attic door and returned outside. He immediately devoured the bread but tried to savor each sweet bite of one of the apples. He stuffed the rest of the fruit inside his shirt for the others at Malka's house, the elastic waistband holding all of it in place.

As he lay in the attic, Noike thought about his meeting with Anna. He could not understand how the Russian woman and her grandson could simply move into his home, sleep in their beds, eat from their dishes. The house had been in his family since before Noike was born, before his mother was even born. He imagined the old woman and her grandson walking through each room, inspecting all of their newly acquired possessions, rejoicing in the death of Maciejow's Jews.

When the orchard workers left the farm, Noike crawled down from the attic and made his way back to the main street, which was now filled with people coming and going to different parts of town. Most of the faces were unfamiliar to Noike—farmers and laborers from neighboring villages, carrying on as if it was an ordinary Sunday. While waiting to cross the street Noike saw a horse and wagon coming towards him on his left. Suddenly, he heard a chorus of boys screaming, "Jew! Jew!"

Noike tried to remain calm, turned around, and started walking in the opposite direction. But a group of boys had jumped from the wagon, ready for a chase. He recognized one of them, Olek Krajewski, a fourteen-year-old who lived next to his grandfather. Anna, the young girl he had seen on the corner, was friendly with his family. He wondered if she had told Olek about their encounter.

Noike turned into an alleyway between two houses and started running as fast as he could. Most of the fruit inside his shirt tumbled to the ground; the precious apples and pears bruised as they crashed into the alley walls. He had made it to a small gate at the other end of the alley when a boy grabbed him by his shirt and said, "I got you!" in Ukrainian. It was an older boy from his school who was known as a tough guy, the school bully. He was almost twice the size of Noike.

Noike reached for his pocket knife and stuck it out from under his clothes, making it look like a pistol. "Are you letting me go or not?" Noike asked, tightening his grip. His heart pounded violently, nervous that the boy would realize there was no gun. Noike had never held a real gun before but he had played with a toy one during the Russian occupation.

"Hey, you know I didn't mean it," the bully said, looking down at the disguised weapon. He released his grip and began to step away from Noike.

Noike turned away from the boy and continued running down the side street, breathing hard as he wondered how his classmates and neighbors could betray him. They had lived together in peace his entire life: he had Polish and Ukrainian friends at school; his mother had cordial relations with all of their neighbors and the customers at her store. The only time he sensed conflict was on Easter Sunday: "Stay away from the Ukrainian church today," his mother would gently warn, knowing that the priest stirred up the local population with impassioned sermons about Jews drinking Christian children's blood, an anti-Semitic tale dating as far back as the Middle Ages.

When Noike reached the *rebbe's* street, he looked over his shoulder, making sure no one was following him back to the house. If the boys were behind him he told himself he would run past the house, even if it meant getting caught. With the street deserted and the boys nowhere to be seen, he dashed back into Malka's house and crawled through the hole into the hiding place. Minutes later, he heard the boys from the wagon running past the house, shouting, "Where are you, Jew? Come out, Jew!" Eventually they must have given up their search and headed home for Sunday dinner.

About three days had passed when Noike and the others heard loud banging noises coming from the house next door, Yosi's former home. Lifting the edge of the cloth covering one of the windows, they could see Ukrainian firemen, the *pozarnie*, who wore brass helmets with their brigade insignia and carried massive hatchets. The brigade was led by one of the Suchetsky boys who lived near Noike's grandfather. The firemen were going from house to house, making sure no one was inside and then boarding up the windows and doors. The local government was trying to discourage squatters since they wanted to distribute Jewish homes to their constituents in an orderly manner.

A short time passed before two firemen entered Malka's house.

Noike and the others could hear the firemen walking from room to room, searching for a hiding place. They prayed the firemen would simply board up the windows and leave but one man stopped in front of the armoire blocking the original door to the hiding place. The fireman shoved the armoire aside and tapped against the freshly painted wall. Suddenly, a hatchet crashed through the wall, scattering bits of plaster and dust throughout the two rooms.

The bright morning light started to pour into the hiding place.

Noike rushed towards the window, pushed it open, and started to climb out, leaving his shoes, hat, and coat behind. He had no idea where to go—it didn't matter at that moment, his body simply propelled him forward, telling him to move, to get out of that place immediately. He saw Srulek stop to put his shoes on and strap the laces.

"Srulek, we don't have time—we have to get out now!" Noike cried.

Srulek and the others continued to get dressed as Noike crawled out the window, into the narrow space between Malka's house and the one next door. The space was so narrow that he had to flatten his body and walk sideways, his lean ten-year-old body barely making it through. He looked down as he stepped into the front yard, convinced that someone would grab him, but his escape path was wide open.

People started shouting "Jews! Jews!" but their eyes were fixed on the other side of the house. Noike looked in that direction and saw a mob of at least ten people, mostly peasant women, gathered around the entrance to Malka's house. "Jews! Jews!" the women squawked, like a flock of crows circling a dead animal. The women pushed each other as they clawed at the front door, hungry for their own share of the kill. They were eager to partake in the pillage, to get a pair of silk stockings, a dressing gown, a set of curtains.

Noike continued to move away from Malka's house, inching towards the sidewalk. When he reached the road leading out of town, he began running. He passed the post office, the lumber mill—he ran by all of the places he had considered part of his home. He continued to run until he reached an empty stretch of pasture about a half mile outside of town. Catching his breath, he slowed down and took in his surroundings.

Noike was on the road that connected Maciejow to Luboml, a market town about thirteen miles west. Between Maciejow and Luboml were vast stretches of pasture and fields growing wheat, groats, or sugar beets. Golden wheat usually covered this stretch of road in the early fall but the Germans had ordered the Ukrainian farmers to harvest it earlier than usual. They wanted to make sure there would be no place for the Jews to run and hide. Every few miles one lone farmhouse, or a small cluster of farmhouses, would suddenly emerge.

Noike had never walked this road alone; he had rarely left Maciejow during the first ten years of his life. Once he had gone with his mother to the nearby market town of Kovel to buy fabric. And on special occasions his family would take the train to Luboml, his grandfather's hometown, to visit relatives. He suddenly felt older, stronger as he walked along the road, but he was still a little boy, his features round, his voice high, his limbs not fully grown. He could feel each stone press into the soft skin on his bare feet. He was not yet used to walking barefoot like some of the farm boys; his paternal grandfather's family owned the local shoe store.

Hunger pangs began to strike; the adrenaline had worn off.

After walking a few miles outside Maciejow, Noike came upon a field of sugar beets; their bright yellow flowers gently swayed in the wind. He knelt down and pulled one from the ground, dusting the loose dirt off with his hand. As he bit into the sweet root, he saw a young man in farm clothes coming from the neighboring village of Bilitch. The man was unarmed but he looked like someone the police would recruit, like one of young men from Gitel's basement. Noike tossed the beet aside and stared into the field, focusing on the flowers, as he waited until the man had passed.

Bilitch, a village known for its nationalistic fervor, was a breeding ground for the local Ukrainian police force. It was the last place Noike wanted to visit but he recalled his aunts talking about Tomke, a Ukrainian farmer in Bilitch who was hiding Jews in his barn. Noike had been to the farm a few times over the years. He usually went with his teenaged aunt, Hanka, who was friends with Tomke's daughter.

Noike got back onto the road and continued walking until he came upon the farm, an isolated plot far from the others in the village. Tomke was chopping wood in the yard, straining as he added each log to a pile along the side of the house. Noike crawled into a tangle of bushes and rustled the leaves to get his attention. Tomke stopped what he was doing, turned, and slowly approached the bushes.

"What are you doing here?" Tomke asked in Ukrainian, immediately recognizing Noike. "It's very dangerous for you to be out right now."

"They killed everyone in Maciejow," he explained. "Can I hide here for a little while?"

"Let me talk to my wife," Tomke said with a worried look. "Wait here for a moment."

When Tomke returned a few minutes later, he told Noike that it was too risky to stay on his farm. His son-in-law was a fervent Ukrainian Nationalist who had collaborated with the Germans during the past *aktions*. He didn't live on the farm but often came over for Sunday dinner. If he discovered Noike on the farm, Tomke was certain the son-in-law would hand him over to the Germans.

"Son, you should go to Luboml—they haven't killed the Jews."

"But I don't know how to get there," Noike said, devastated that he could not hide on the farm. He was scared to be alone on the open road when nighttime came, without food, water, or a place to sleep. The journey on foot could take a half a day or more.

"Stay off the main road. You should cut through the fields behind Bilitch." Tomke pointed towards a harvested swath of wheat. "Then walk along the railroad tracks which pass through Luboml."

Noike seemed to have no other choice. He followed Tomke's instructions, winding his way through the fields, until he found the narrow dirt road that ran along the tracks. He had been walking for several miles when an old farmer passed by on a horse-pulled wagon loaded with straw. Waving his hands in the air, Noike called out for a ride in Ukrainian.

"Where are you headed?" the farmer asked, sizing up the curious looking hitchhiker who was barefoot like a peasant, yet dressed like a Jew.

"*Pan*, I'm going to Luboml," Noike said, "or as far as you'll take me."

"All right, jump in the back!" the old man said, waving him on board.

When they got onto the road, the farmer gave Noike a thick slice of rye bread with ham. "*Budlaska*, please eat," he said with much enthusiasm, perhaps sensing that his young passenger was hungry. "My wife baked the bread fresh this morning—I already had plenty," he patted his big belly.

"*Pan*, thank you," Noike said as he accepted the bread and forbidden food. Good Jewish boys, he had been taught, weren't supposed to eat pork.

He brought the meat to his lips but it was as if a magnet was pulling it away from his mouth. Not wanting to insult the farmer, he ate the bread and stuffed the meat into his pocket.

They had been on the road for a few miles when they reached a crossroads: one road went through the woods; the other passed through the village of Podhorodne then continued on towards Luboml. The farmer told Noike that it was time to part ways since he was headed in the other direction. Noike hopped off the wagon and started walking towards Podhorodne.

Podhorodne was about the same size as Bilitch. Noike had never been to the village but he thought the thatched homes looked peaceful and safe in the midday sun. He walked down the road and approached the first home he came across: a one-room farmhouse with a front yard overflowing with fruit trees. Through the front screen door he saw a young woman working away in the kitchen; she was wearing a white cotton blouse and a long, checkered blue skirt.

"*Pani*, can I have something to eat?" Noike asked in Ukrainian. He had not been taught to beg but he was tired, hungry, and desperate.

"*Vitayemo*," she welcomed him as she removed her apron and smoothed her skirt. "Please, sit down—you can have some fruit from our orchard." She had a fresh, rosy face and wore her butter blonde hair in a low bun.

Noike sat quietly, trying not to eat the fruit too quickly. He could hear his mother's voice in his head, telling him to be polite to the lady, not to eat with his mouth open. He was not used to being in a stranger's home without his mother, brother, or sister.

The woman smiled gently at Noike. She must have known that he was from Maciejow: many villagers had advance warning about the raids. Some learned from family members who were in the police, others learned from the Germans who sought their cooperation in return for extra rations. Sensing that he had been left on his own, she offered to help him out.

"There's a family down the road who could use a shepherd to pasture their cows," the young woman said. "Would you like to meet them?"

Noike had never pastured a cow in his life but he was worried that everyone would be killed when he got to Luboml, that he would have to find a new family. Not wanting to be left alone, he agreed to meet the farmers.

A half a mile down the road they came upon another Ukrainian farmhouse, this one bordered by several fenced-in pens of livestock: sheep, pigs, and a lone cow. Dozens of chickens and a few geese were running loose in the front yard. The woman opened the gate leading to the house, which was painted white with bright blue trim and a pale yellow door.

"*Dobry dien,*" she said as they walked inside.

"*Dobry dien,* Mariya," the farmer and his wife replied. They appeared to be old friends; the young woman embraced the couple as they said their hellos.

"I have a visitor," she said, glancing at Noike. "Can we talk in private?"

"Yes, of course. Let me give this young man a glass of milk first," the wife said, smiling as she offered the fresh milk to Noike.

They stepped out into the yard and began talking.

Noike looked around the room as he drank the milk. The house had a smooth, clay floor—common in many of the older farmhouses—and sturdy pieces of furniture made from the local pine. Except for a holy picture of the Madonna and child, few decorations adorned the walls. Noike had seen the Madonna image before but did not know its significance.

Within moments he saw the farmers shake hands and come back into the house wearing broad smiles. "We want to keep you on our farm," the couple started to explain. "But to make sure it's OK, we want to take you to the *batushka*, the priest, to bless you first."

Noike imagined his *rebbe*, his teacher of Hebrew and religion, wagging his long, skinny finger at him: *You are a Jew! What are you doing, child?* He was suddenly frightened by the woman, the couple, and the priest he would never meet. He was not ready to give up his old life, to become part of this family, to practice their religion.

"*Duzhe dzakuyu,*" he thanked everyone as he stood up and hurried towards the door. "But I need to go to Luboml to meet my cousins."

## 9

## ONE OF OURS
### Florida. May 2006

"What do you want for breakfast today?" my father asked upon my return to Florida. "I can make scrambled eggs, pancakes, *challah* French toast—whatever you like."

"Breakfast?" I frowned, eager to go through all of the questions I had accumulated since my last visit. We had been in constant communication via email, phone, and even letters, but it could not fully replace our in-person meetings.

"I'll make cream cheese omelets," he said with a nod.

"Dad, I already ate something. I usually don't eat a big breakfast."

"Well, I like to start with a big breakfast." My dad smiled as he took the eggs, milk, cream cheese, and butter out of the refrigerator.

People often say that my father got the "Jewish mother" gene, referring to his tendency to encourage eating. When I was younger he would exhibit this trait around my immediate family but also around my girlfriends. Sleepover parties at my house meant elaborate ice cream sundaes at bedtime and fresh-cooked breakfast in the morning.

An hour or so later, after he had polished off his trademark cream cheese omelet, finished his coffee, and scanned the New York Times, we started our research.

"Dad, can you explain where Malka's house was in relation to your house?"

"Ah," he raised a finger. "Wait a moment."

He returned with a folder containing photos and sketches of Maciejow. The sketches were drawn partially from memory, then filled in with information he had gathered over the years. He had marked many of the homes, businesses, and synagogues, drawing arrows to indicate how he had walked from one place to the other.

"Here's a photo of that alley I ran down when that boy was chasing me," my father said, leafing through the folder. The photo, a dark alley littered with a few crumbling bricks, had no meaning to anyone but him before now.

In 1993 he returned to Maciejow for the first time in almost fifty years. The trip was organized by another survivor from his town who had arranged to have monuments erected on the mass graves behind the former German headquarters, near the lime mines, and in the woods.

"The mayor of Lukiv gave a speech before they unveiled the monument at the lime mines," my father explained. He showed me a photo of a middle-aged man in a gray suit surrounded by farmers and women in traditional Ukrainian dress. Maciejow had been renamed to "Lukiv" when it became part of Ukraine after the war. "Here's a close-up that shows the inscription on the monument," he said, handing me another photo. He translated the inscription, which was written in both Hebrew and Russian:

> *4,500 Jews from Maciejow (Lukiv) and the vicinity were brutally murdered and buried here by the Nazis and their collaborators. This monument was erected in their memory and in the memory of other anonymous people who didn't receive a proper burial.*

The mayor called on a few locals to make more speeches, including the daughter of the Ukrainian farmers who had saved Rubin Grosser, the boy who crawled out of the lime mines. My father met Rubin Grosser in New York City many years ago but he never heard about his experience at the lime mines; Rubin never mentioned it. When the official speeches were finished, my father found himself drawn to an old Ukrainian woman standing in the crowd. She was bent over and wore a babushka over her snow-white hair.

"Were you here during the war?" my father asked.

She nodded her head, then explained that she was born in the town.

"*I* was here in 1942," my father said, pointing at his chest.

The old woman crossed herself. "That little blonde boy," she said, suddenly reflecting back to the war. "He was such a beautiful boy. We told them, 'Leave him alone, he's just a baby.' But they shot him as he ran away. They shot him once again before he fell to the ground."

"*Who* shot him?" my father pressed. He had been bothered by some of the official speeches. They had rightfully demonized the Nazis for what they did to the Jews, but they did not admit any wrongdoing on the part of their countrymen.

"It was one of ours," the old woman said, her eyes downcast.

WHILE WALKING THROUGH THE TOWN LATER THAT DAY, my father was approached by another Ukrainian, an older man who had lived in Maciejow in 1942. He must have recognized my father from the ceremony at the lime mines.

"I saw what they did to the blacksmith," the old man said, anxious to tell his story, to remove a weight he had carried around for many years. "He refused to denounce your God so they gouged his eyes out."

"*Who* did?" my father asked again.

"One of ours," the man replied, shaking his head.

My father told me that he felt some consolation after hearing these stories. They were horrific but at least they were honest; the storytellers did not selectively edit their memories. He then showed me a picture taken of him at the lime mines. Dressed in a dark suit and tie, he is standing in front of the monument where his mother, sister, and many other friends and family were killed. The sky is filled with ominous looking clouds; mountains of white lime from the mines blend into the background. His fists are clenched as he looks towards the ground, fighting back tears.

## 10

# DEAR BROTHERS
*Luboml, Poland. October, 1942*

A crew of young Jewish men were laying railroad ties when Noike reached the outskirts of Luboml. German soldiers were standing nearby, barking orders and crashing their whips if the men didn't move fast enough. Noike was desperate to talk to the men but terrified of the soldiers. They would have known about the *aktion* in Maciejow and would be quick to silence a survivor. Noike moved into the pasture next to the tracks and continued walking towards Luboml. At least he knew some Jews were still alive.

The center of Luboml was no longer the bustling hub of activity that Noike remembered. All of the shops surrounding the main square were shuttered; only a few people were walking around its perimeter. One of them was a young woman with auburn hair; she was wearing a smart, wool coat with a "Star of David" armband—a clear sign that she was safe to approach.

"Excuse me, lady, do you know where I can find Falik Ginzburg's house?" Noike asked in his most polite Yiddish.

Falik was one of his paternal grandfather's brothers and a well-established businessman who owned a fabric store, a pub, a soda factory, and a candy store. Noike's favorite place to visit had been the candy store. They sold all of the typical sweets—chocolates, suckers, licorice—but the homemade ice cream sandwiches were their crowning glory. Noike would stand at the counter, watching closely as one of the girls in the shop assembled the sandwiches using a wooden mold. She would put one wafer in the bottom of the mold, add vanilla ice cream, then cover it with another wafer. She would then push the little handle, and voila, the sandwich would pop out of the mold. Noike would take each bite slowly, savoring the special treat.

"*Gutn ovent*," the woman in the square greeted him in Yiddish. "How do you know Falik Ginzburg?"

"I'm Noike Ginzburg, one of his nephews from Maciejow."

"You're Falik's nephew!" She leaned back to get a better look at him. With his soiled clothing and dirty feet, at first glance Noike appeared to be a beggar boy, but his deep blue eyes and delicate features were clearly those of a Ginzburg. "We are *mishpokhe*—we are the same family, Noikele. Last year I married Yankel Ginzburg, Falik's youngest son. My name is Basia."

Many couples continued with marriage plans early on in the war, but they were small affairs: a quick ceremony in someone's living room, maybe a cake if they could buy the hard-to-find ingredients on the black market. Noike vaguely recalled his mother mentioning this marriage.

"We need to move fast since it's almost evening curfew," Basia said, glancing down at her watch. "I have to get to the *apteka* before it closes—my baby boy needs some medicine—but my brother, Isaac, can take you to Falik's house. Wait here a moment while I get him."

Basia soon returned with Isaac, a slender boy in his mid-twenties who walked with his shoulders back and his head held high in the air. He was wearing a newsboy cap cocked at an angle; bits and pieces of his dark, wavy hair peeked out from underneath.

"You must be tired," Isaac said, putting his hand on Noike's shoulder. "I heard you traveled all the way from Maciejow—that's at least thirteen miles!"

Noike nodded his head as they wound their way around the square.

Isaac explained how Luboml had changed since the war broke out. The town used to have more than five thousand people, most of them Jewish. Some Jews fled to Russia when the Germans crossed the nearby Bug River in 1941, but the majority of the population stayed behind. Within days of the occupation, the SS established two ghettos: one had working Jews who carried "gold passes," so named because they typically required a pay-off to the German authorities; the other had older people and children who carried "white passes." The north side of the market and Falik's house were both in the ghetto where people carried "gold passes."

Ghettos were a means to separate Jews from the non-Jewish population. Jews were further divided within the ghetto walls in order to facilitate deportation to the killing centers. Non-worker groups were liquidated before the worker groups, that way the Germans could use the workers to "clean up" after the *aktion*. The "clean up" included collecting, sorting, and cleaning possessions left by the dead. At least one million Jews would be forced into ghettos during the war.

"Ah, here we are," Isaac said, pointing to a large, three-storey house with its curtains drawn. Isaac placed two fingers on the *mezuzah* and kissed them before walking through the door; Noike stood on his tiptoes and did the same.

Three generations of Ginzburgs had lived in the house before the war. Falik, his wife, and their three daughters lived on the second and third floors. Kalman, their eldest son, was stricken with polio and confined to the first floor with his wife and two children. The number of residents in the house ballooned when the massacres started in the neighboring towns. Dozens of Falik's relatives had come to the house seeking shelter; no one was turned away.

Noike was surprised to find two of his young aunts from Maciejow, Sabina and Fania, the same aunts who were hiding in the attic when the SS had raided his grandfather's house in the middle on the night. They had known Noike from the time he was born and used to take turns watching him when his mother was busy running the fabric store.

"Noikele, you escaped!" Sabina said, covering her mouth with both hands. Sabina and Fania had been in Luboml for several days and assumed there were no other survivors from the *aktion* in Maciejow.

"Where's the rest of your family?" Fania added, not accustomed to seeing young Noike all alone. "Weren't all of you together?"

Noike told them how his mother and brother were captured in Gitel Silverberg's basement and how he fled Maciejow when the *rebbe*'s house was discovered by the firemen. When he told the story about his mother, it was as if he never left the basement. He could still clearly see the Ukrainian police in their black uniforms, leading his mother away.

Sabina and Fania tried to embrace Noike—to comfort him like they used to when he was younger—but he stiffened at their maternal touch, not wanting to be treated like a child anymore. He was unaware that he was still a vulnerable little boy, no matter how old and hardened he felt inside.

"When did you leave Maciejow?" Noike asked. In the days leading up to the *aktion*, everyone in town was scrambling to find hiding places. Noike did not know where most of his extended family had gone, and was eager to connect all of their stories. If his aunts had survived, maybe others in his family had also escaped.

Sabina and Fania explained how they had come to Luboml.

While Noike was hiding in the basement with his mother, Sabina, Fania, and Hanka, their younger sister, trekked into the forest outside Maciejow, where an old Ukrainian man had promised them shelter. When they arrived the man showed them the hiding place: a shallow earth pit under a haystack. Having no other alternatives, the girls stepped down and lay on their stomachs, covering their faces as the old man pushed the haystack back into place. Insects from the haystack soon descended upon the girls, crawling towards their faces. The girls squeezed their eyes and mouths shut, tried to swat the creatures away. When the sky grew dark, they crawled out from under the haystack and roamed the woods in search of food and water. They subsisted on rainwater and wild plums for a few days, then decided to leave the woods. Sabina and Fania went to Luboml, while Hanka went to Tomke's farm in Bilitch. Tomke had agreed hide Hanka but he would not take all three sisters: Hanka, with her light hair and strong Polish skills, could pass as a Pole if discovered; the others could not.

"*I* went to Tomke's farm," Noike said.

"Hanka must have been there," they said. "You didn't see her?"

"No, he told me it was too dangerous to stay there."

Noike also learned that his grandmother came to Luboml before the raids and was staying with her sister-in-law, who lived in the non-worker ghetto. Although he longed to visit his grandmother, it was too dangerous to move from one ghetto to another. His grandfather, Yakob Ginzburg, was too ill to travel and had stayed behind in another hiding place in Maciejow.

Sabina led Noike to the kitchen and prepared him a plate of food. As he stood near the kitchen window, he heard a group of men reciting the *Sukkot* prayers. *Sukkot*, held on the fifth day after *Yom Kippur*, commemorates the forty-year period when the Israelites wandered the desert, living in temporary shelters. Stepping into the yard between Falik's house and the one next door, Noike discovered a *sukkah*, a small hut of branches and leaves, built to celebrate the holiday.

*What are they doing? We are getting killed and they are celebrating Sukkot!*

After the prayers were over, Noike approached his great uncles—Falik and Yosel—who were sharing a plate of food in the *sukkah*. Falik and Yosel were observant Jews like their older brother, Yakob Ginzburg, but they did not wear long beards or *tzitzis*, fringe worn on the four corners of Jewish men's garments. Instead they wore tailored European suits and fedoras and had their hair cut in the latest styles. There were six other siblings in their immediate family: Berel, Avram, Faige, Hinda, Tzirel, and Raisel. In the 1920s, Hinda emigrated to the United States and Tzirel emigrated to Argentina; the rest of them lived in Luboml, Maciejow, and other nearby towns.

Noike told his uncles what he had experienced in Maciejow, hoping they could prevent the same thing from happening in Luboml.

"We have built hiding places, Noike," Falik explained. He always had a calm demeanor, no matter what the circumstances.

"But we had hiding places in Maciejow—they didn't help us for very long!" Noike feverishly listed all of the hiding places that had been discovered, all of the people who had been captured.

"Noike, don't worry, we are making preparations," his uncle Yosel added, wiping his mouth with a white, cotton kerchief. "Come, sit with us in the *sukkah*," he patted the chair next to him.

Neither Yosel nor Falik wanted to worry their young nephew. They were well aware that things would get worse in Luboml but they did not know precisely when or how. And even if they had every last detail, they could not imagine what it would feel like, what they would actually do, when the madness ensued. Noike, having experienced the *aktion* in Maciejow, knew better than anyone.

Noike could hardly get out of bed the next morning—his feet were badly bruised and swollen from the long walk to Luboml. When he tried to stand he was reminded of the rocks and pebbles that had dug into his feet for mile after mile. He spent most of the day lying on one of the spare beds crammed into the living room.

"Noikele, I have some clothes for you," Falik's wife said, placing a pile on the edge of his bed: a suit coat, a wool hat, and most importantly, a pair of socks and lace-up shoes. She was a plump woman in her fifties with thick, black hair that she swept back from her face and held with pins.

"Thank you, *Tante*," Noike said.

"Your cousin Hanna will come to the house later today. Basia must have told them you had come. She'll take you to see your *Tante* Gitel." Gitel and Noike's mother were sisters.

Hanna arrived in the afternoon as planned. She was a vibrant young woman in her early twenties who had a beautiful voice, like a *chazzan*, the person who leads prayers in the synagogue. Before the war, when Noike's family visited Gitel's home on *Shabbat*, Hanna's father would encourage her to sing the *zmirot*, the traditional Sabbath songs. She always hesitated at first, embarrassed by the attention, but eventually she would sing for everyone. Noike knew her better than most of his Luboml cousins since she had stayed at their home while recovering from an illness a few years earlier.

As they cut through the streets of Luboml and walked past the former market and one of the older synagogues, Hanna asked Noike what had happened in Maciejow. He told her about hiding in the basement and the *rebbe*'s house, and how everyone around him had been captured and taken to the lime mines.

"But maybe they escaped," she said, gripping his hand tightly, holding back tears.

Noike looked down and said nothing.

"The Jewish resistance is rounding up guns, Noike," she said, trying to lift his spirits. "We plan to escape to the woods."

Jewish resistance groups sprung up in ghettos all over Europe. Brought together by their associations with political or religious movements, many of the members were youths who could withstand the harsh life in the woods. Early resistance acts were often non-violent: underground newspapers, clandestine prayer, or secret Hebrew schools. Armed resistance became more common as news spread about the ghetto liquidations. With death imminent, many felt they had nothing to lose.

"Where is everyone, Noikele?" his aunt Gitel asked when they arrived at the house. She had the same gentle mannerisms as his mother but was several years older, with deep wrinkles lining her eyes and mouth.

Noike told her the same stories he had told Hanna.

Gitel broke into tears. She had lost her daughter and three grandchildren when the *Einsatzgruppen* descended upon the town of Kovel a few months earlier.

"Noikele, you must be hungry," Hanna said, wrapping an arm around Gitel and leading her into the kitchen. "We'll make you something to eat."

As he waited on the living room couch, Noike could hear Gitel quietly weeping in the kitchen as Hanna tried to console her. He thought he, too, should be crying for the loss of his family. But it was as if something inside of him had broken, severing his ability to cry, to grieve, to mourn. Tears would not come for a long time.

It took a moment for Noike to realize that the young man standing in Falik's doorway and covered in a thin layer of gray dust was his brother, Herschel. Still wearing the same clothes from Gitel Silverberg's basement, Noike thought he must be a ghost as he stared at the figure; he had never imagined that anyone could survive the lime mines. He called out his brother's name, expecting the vision to disappear, but his brother stepped forward and pulled Noike towards him.

"Where have you been? I thought you were dead!" Noike said bitterly as he leaned heavily against his brother's chest. He wanted to see his family more than anything but he was angry, confused, and unsure what to do, how to feel. Should he be mourning, hopeful, still running for his life?

"Noike, settle down, I thought you were dead too!" Herschel said, trying to calm his little brother. He then explained how he escaped Maciejow during the *aktion*.

Herschel was marched to the synagogue, along with the dozens of other Jews who had been captured in Gitel's basement. Herschel and another boy were pushed towards the back of the synagogue, near the large stove used to heat the building during the winter months. While the police were focused on the new arrivals in the front of the synagogue, the two boys looked around for a way out. The front and side doors were heavily guarded and the windows were too high to reach without anyone noticing. Suddenly their eyes fell on the massive wood stove, which had not been used all summer.

"Stand up!" one of the policemen ordered.

Herschel and the other boy crouched down and crept towards the stove, safely hidden behind the rows of people who were now standing. Herschel jumped into the stove first, then helped pull the other boy into its long, dark chamber. On all fours, they moved towards the back of the stove, then stood up inside the chimney. Clouds of dust and black sheets of soot fell from the chimney as their bodies squeezed into the space.

"*Vilezai!*" they heard a policeman yell. "Get out!"

The officer walked over to the stove and pointed his rifle inside. "*Vilezai!*" he called again, knocking the rifle against the inside of the stove. The boys knew that they could be killed either way; they would not move. The officer stuck his head inside but saw nothing; it was pitch black and too narrow for a grown man to crawl through. "*Holera!*" he cursed into the darkness, before firing several rounds. He had some success: the other boy was struck in the chest, collapsing at the base of the chimney; Hershel had a superficial wound in his foot.

"Does it still hurt?" Noike asked. "Let me see it."

"Nah, it's just a little sore," Herschel said, removing his shoe and sock. It was no longer bleeding but there was a small gash and dried blood where the bullet had ripped through the skin. Noike touched it gently.

Herschel remained still inside the stove, hoping the police officer would assume he was dead like the other boy; no one had bothered to remove the young victims. A short time later, he heard muffled bits of Yiddish from another part of the room: "Murderers! Child killers!" Their voices disappeared as they were shoved out of the synagogue, their words replaced by footsteps as the police marched them to the lime mines. As each minute passed, Herschel felt relieved that he had managed to escape death, but he also felt sickened: sickened by the fate of his family and neighbors; sickened by the death of the boy slumped next to him.

Herschel stayed in the stove until nighttime, trying to nurse his wound, waiting for the shots from the lime mines to stop. As he sat there listening to each bullet fire, he pictured his friends and neighbors standing at the edge of the mines. He tried to tune out the sounds but it was relentless. Many hours passed before a deadly silence finally settled on the town. He waited another hour, maybe two, then crawled to the stove opening and peeked out into the synagogue hall. It was now empty, quiet; strewn about the hall were the personal belongings left behind: cotton handkerchiefs, scarves, scraps of paper filled with handwritten prayers.

The room still felt warm.

Worried that the police might still be guarding the front and side doors, Herschel crawled through the back window and slipped into the synagogue garden. Stepping quietly on the grass, he scanned the road in front of the synagogue and listened for signs of the police: there was nothing. Ducking behind houses, fences, and bushes, he managed to make it to the garden behind their grandfather's house. When he paused to take some vegetables, he heard shouting from one of the Ukrainian neighbors: "If you don't get out of here, I'll call the Germans," the young woman warned as she stormed out of her house.

Herschel was shocked by the betrayal, the hateful threat. The woman had been kind to his family in the past; she even had children almost the same age as him. He took one final look at Maciejow before he ran through the field, not stopping until he felt certain that no one was around him. When he finally reached the main road, he started the long walk to Luboml.

"Blimele was in the synagogue too," Herschel said once he finished his story.

"Did you see her?" Noike asked.

"No, no I didn't," Herschel lowered his gaze. "But she left us a message."

As he knelt in the back of the synagogue, Herschel's eyes were drawn to the wall where previous victims had left messages to their loved ones, or had simply written their names. Scanning the messages, he was haunted by one scratched deep into the plaster: *Meine teyere brider, ich beit n'kumeh fur myr*. My dear brothers, take revenge. Below the message, written in the same hand, was Blimele's name.

She was a good-natured soul; she must have seen or experienced some horrible atrocities to have written that message. Noike imagined that his sister had been captured but to hear the story from Herschel made it certain, final. Although Noike was the youngest, he had always felt protective of his older sister. When the Germans first occupied Maciejow, he often volunteered to go to the local water pump, worried that the soldiers would take advantage of a pretty young girl like Blima. He wished he could have done something to save her.

Noike went on to tell Herschel what had happened in Gitel Silverberg's basement with their mother, stopping with the story of how he found his way to Luboml. He told him what their mother had done to save his life, and how helpless he had felt when they took her away. Herschel shared his grief but neither of them could mourn for their mother, their sister, and the countless others who perished. Mourning meant you dropped your guard and had become vulnerable. Mourning was dangerous.

That night, Herschel and Noike shared the bed in the living room, holding each other tightly as they had done the night the SS raided their grandfather's home. "I'll never leave you again," Herschel said just before they went to sleep. Noike looked up at Herschel's face. His eyebrow still had the scar from when Noike had hit him years earlier. It was an accident—they had been horsing around in the yard—but he still felt bad. He wished it never had happened; he wished many things had never happened.

# 11

## FINDING BLIMELE
*New York, circa 1980*

My father's office was the only room in my childhood home where the door was kept shut. He would go down there in the evenings or on weekends and work away on a project unknown to me, eventually coming back upstairs for a much anticipated ice cream break. After coming home one afternoon from a day at junior high school in the fall of 1980, I found myself drawn to this seemingly forbidden room.

Slowly, I turned the knob and leaned my right arm into the door, giving it some pressure since it would usually stick. When it finally opened, it sounded like someone gasping for air. Even in the early afternoon it seemed like nighttime in that room: the patterned shades were always drawn shut; the ceiling light bulb was burnt out. On the left wall were bookcases filled with World Book encyclopedias, engineering textbooks, and my mom's old paperback novels—Harlequin romances, spy stories, mysteries. The right side of the room had a large closet with a sliding door—behind it was my secret hiding place, only used in the final rounds of hide-and-seek.

In the middle of the room was my father's desk, shrouded in darkness.

I moved to turn on the dusty lamp, illuminating no more than a foot or two of the desk space. Among the piles of bills, notepads, and old newspaper clippings, I noticed a black and white photograph special enough for my father to remove it from the albums and boxes in the upstairs closet. The picture looked like the class photos we took at school every year, but there were twice as many students, and it was old and faded. The class stood under a tree, in front of a white picket fence.

Holding the corners with both of my hands, I examined each child's facial expression, hairstyle, and clothing. Many of the boys wore dark shorts with suspenders; light cotton shirts were neatly tucked in. Newsboy caps—

the same kind I had seen in old movies with my mother—seemed popular with some of the boys. Most of the girls had freshly trimmed bangs and chin-length bobs; others wore long braids. They, too, were dressed neatly, wearing cotton dresses or skirts with button-down blouses.

Scanning each row, I searched for my father in the sea of faces, but none of the little boys resembled him. Flipping over the image, I searched for clues—a name, a message, a date—but nothing was written on the other side.

I put the photo back under the pile on his desk.

Sometime later, one weekday evening or weekend, I followed my father when he went downstairs to his office. As he sat at the desk sorting through a stack of bills, I looked over his shoulder, and pointed at the old photo sticking out from under the papers.

"Where's that photo from?" I asked.

"Maciejow—it's a Hebrew school photo," he said, sliding his reading glasses down his nose as he glanced my way. He picked up the photo and handed it to me.

I looked at the photo again, as if it were the first time.

"That's my sister," he added, pointing at the girl sitting in the middle of the first row as he continued to shuffle through the bills.

The photo began to take on a different meaning: I was named after Blimele. Her name was never mentioned while I was growing up, so for years I assumed her name was Suzanne, which means "Lily," or Shoshanna—my Hebrew name—which means "Rose." Blima or Blimele simply means "Flower."

"How old was she here?"

"She was in kindergarten," he replied, briefly looking back up.

Blimele was sitting behind two boys, making it difficult to see her clothing. Strands of her long blond hair appeared to be pulled back and tied with ribbon. My grandmother, or great-grandmother, must have tied that ribbon, helped picked out her little dress. Her eyes were closed, almost meditative.

I knew she had been killed, yet it seemed impossible: she was a child, just like me. Many, if not all, of the other children in that photo must have also been killed, along with their teachers. Had I been alive back then, they would have killed me too.

For years this was the only image I had of Blimele—the innocent schoolgirl with ribbons in her hair. When I learned how she had cut her hair to look younger, how she had died, and what her last message to the world had been, she was transformed into a fierce young woman. Her eyes were no longer closed; her blue eyes were wide open and saying, "Avenge me. Avenge all of us."

# 12

## THE RAID

*Luboml, Poland. October, 1942*

A few days after Herschel arrived in Luboml, a riot of gunshots and screams erupted at four in the morning—the *aktion* had begun.

Yankel Ginzburg, Falik's son, had warned everyone in the house that an *aktion* was imminent. He was part of the lumber brigade, a slave labor group that worked in the nearby woods. Yankel and the other brigade members became suspicious when they learned that their work permits would not been renewed. That night, Yankel took his father and uncles to a bunker that brigade members had built in the woods. He planned to bring the rest of the family the next day but the raid happened before he made it back.

Everyone in Falik's house rushed out of bed and frantically made their way to their designated hiding place: the first floor bedroom; the third floor apartment; the attic. Noike and Herschel ran for the bedroom, the largest of the three hiding places. The doorway between the bedroom and the kitchen had been sealed off and repainted, much like the one in Malka's house. A secret entrance had been built into the wood storage bin, a narrow shaft next to the kitchen stove. Noike and Herschel got on their hands and knees and crawled through the bin. Almost twenty of their relatives were already crammed in the room.

One wall inside the hiding place faced the main street and had a row of small windows covered in black cloth. A few people took turns looking outside, lifting a corner of the cloth, careful not to draw any attention. SS officers lined the sidewalks, watching as the Ukrainian police ran through the center of the street, chasing Jews to the synagogue. German Shepherds were set loose; they bit and tore at their victims' legs as they raced through the street.

In one corner of the bedroom, a baby boy started crying. Basia, the woman Noike met when he first arrived in Luboml, was the mother. She had come to the house when her husband left for the woods the night before. She rocked the little boy back and forth and tried to nurse him, but he could not be consoled. Noike was reminded of the *aktion* in Maciejow; it was as if the scene in Gitel Silverberg's basement was happening all over again. But this time the road was filled with an army of SS and police. There was no clear way for the mother or baby to leave without risking capture for everyone.

Noike was not the only one who worried. All of the relatives had heard about his experience in Maciejow, including Basia. As more SS and police entered the area and the baby's cries grew louder, there was pressure to take drastic measures. "Why should we all die?" one asked. "One life could save us all," another said. After a vicious debate, Basia was led away as one of the others smothered the child to death. The baby's shrill cries were soon replaced by the muffled whimpers coming from Basia as she hugged the limp child to her chest and prayed for forgiveness. Everyone in the hiding place bowed their heads and covered their mouths, feeling complicit in the dreadful act.

Silence ensued in the hiding place.

They had been in the bedroom for a few hours when one of the men volunteered to get more water from the barrel in the kitchen. The others encouraged him to wait until the streets emptied out but the man had grown irritable and claustrophobic in the dark, crowded space. Ignoring their pleas, he began pulling the wood out of the bin. Not more than a couple of pieces of wood had been removed when several gunshots flew through the bedroom wall. One bullet sailed right past Noike and Herschel, who were seated next to the entrance.

"Close it! Close it!" everyone inside urged in loud whispers.

"Why close it?" Noike said. "They know we're here—we're trapped! If we come out now, we might be able to escape." It sounded as if there were only one or two policemen in the kitchen. Once the police realized there was a large group, they were more likely to send for reinforcements, making it impossible to overpower them.

Everyone in the hiding place agreed to open the entrance.

Noike crawled through the wood bin and stuck his head into the kitchen. Standing directly in front of him was a Ukrainian policeman, pointing a rifle in his direction. He appeared to be in his early twenties and was wearing the same black uniform as the men who had raided Gitel's basement. He pushed Noike back inside.

"Collect the gold and bring it back to me," he demanded in Ukrainian.

Noike silently crawled back into the hiding space.

"They want gold," Noike reported.

One of the men removed his black fedora and passed it around the perimeter of the hiding place. Noike averted his eyes as his relatives parted with their most sentimental possessions: their wedding bands, a watch from a grandfather, a locket from a grandmother. Once the hat made its way around the room, Noike crawled back through the bin and handed it to the police officer. Another officer entered the room, also armed with a rifle.

As the two men divided up the loot, Noike started to climb out of the storage bin again. He turned to see if Herschel was behind him but his brother sat motionless, the memories of the Ukrainian police in Maciejow still fresh in his mind. Noike, on the other hand, was somehow emboldened by his encounters with the police, determined to escape from them again. He grabbed Herschel by the hair and pulled him until he came out of the bin.

Glancing through the kitchen window, Noike spotted the stairway landing that led to the second floor of the house. About a foot below the window stood a woodpile, stacked high enough to reach the window sill. Noike started to walk towards the pile and motioned to Herschel to do the same. Suddenly, one of the Ukrainian policemen noticed that the boys had moved. He raised his gun and pointed it at Noike.

"Get away from there, or I'll shoot you like a dog," his face darkened.

Noike reached for the fountain pen in his pocket and extended it towards the officer, naively hoping it might appease him, might convince the police to let them go. Falik had given it to him a couple of days ago.

"You're not going to need that soon," the policeman snarled as he snatched the pen.

At that moment, Noike thought it would be the end for him, for all of them. Now that the men had their gold, the poor Jews would be of no use to them. He imagined marching to the graves in Luboml, standing in front of an open pit, waiting for the guns to fire. As a last resort, he considered stabbing the fountain pen into the officer's eye, giving everyone enough time to run out of the house.

But the police weren't done; they had one more request.

"Go back inside and collect the *karbovanzy*," he ordered this time. *Kar-*

*bovanzy* referred to the Ukrainian currency; the Ukrainian nationalists had introduced it in June of 1942. It was part of their efforts to establish an independent Ukrainian state.

Noike crawled through the storage bin again; Herschel stayed behind with the police. This time, Noike announced that the officers wanted cash. Again he waited as his relatives removed the wads of money they had hidden inside their shoes and clothes and stuffed them into the hat.

Noike came back outside and presented the hat overflowing with *karbovanzy*. The officer's eyes nearly popped out of his head as he grabbed the hat out of Noike's hands. Most of the police came from poor farming families and had never seen that much money. The other police officer came back into the kitchen, carrying silver kiddish cups, torah ornaments, and menorahs from the prayer room.

"Did you check under the floorboards?" the officer with the money asked, stepping into the prayer room. The Ukrainian police had become skilled at searching every nook and cranny of Jewish homes.

While the police were in the prayer room the boys climbed on top of the wood pile and pulled themselves up onto the window sill. Their eyes still fixed on the police, they took their shoes off and swung their legs around to the other side of the sill, then jumped onto the landing, dashed up the stairs, and ran into the second bedroom. Noike hid under the bed against the far wall; Herschel hid behind the bed, close to the door.

Within seconds the police noticed that the boys had disappeared. "Lousy Jews!" one cursed, "Vlodzia, go find them."

The man called Vlodzia ran upstairs to search for the boys. He began with the first bedroom, opening closet doors and then angrily slamming them shut. Finding nothing, he went to the second bedroom and stood in the doorway. From underneath the bed, Noike could see his heavy black boots caked in mud, the pant cuffs of his black uniform, the barrel of the rifle at his side

"Sneaky Jews, running away behind our backs," Vlodzia grunted as he tapped his rifle on the ground.

Noike placed his palms flat on the smooth, hardwood floor and pushed himself closer to the wall.

"I'm gonna find you boys," Vlodzia continued to grumble to himself.

Noike's heart thumped heavily as he held his breath.

The police officer was about to enter the room when his partner called his name, and ordered him to come down. Noike watched as the black boots turned to leave, then heard the boots pounding down the stairs towards the kitchen. When he seemed a safe distance away, Noike crawled out from under the bed and inched closer to his brother.

"Herschel?" Noike whispered softly.

"Shhh…" Herschel said, stepping out from behind the bed. He motioned his head towards the second floor kitchen, directly across from the bedroom.

The boys peeked through the window facing the side of the house and discovered a ledge wide enough for two people. Herschel crawled through first, quietly stepping onto the ledge.

"I can't reach," Noike said, his skinny legs dangling from the window. He was too short to step down and jumping would create too much noise.

Herschel grabbed Noike's legs and guided him onto the ledge; Noike placed his hands on Herschel's shoulders for support. They sat down and took a moment to rest below the window, wondering what to do next.

"You might want to enter through the area over there with the broken tiles," they heard a boy say in Yiddish.

To their right they saw two teenaged Jewish boys pointing at the broken tiles in the roof next door, the Stern's house. The boys were sitting next to the chimney with their knees pulled close to their chests. They explained that the opening led to the attic where other Jews were known to be hiding.

Noike and Herschel crawled across the roof and helped each other through the small opening in the tiles. They landed in an unfinished attic littered with a broken chair and a torn mattress. The boys lay on the mattress, uncertain of their next move.

"Let's see if we can find some food downstairs," Herschel suggested.

They opened the attic door and peered into the main floor of the house. Silence. No sign of the police, the Stern family, or other Jews. The boys climbed down the ladder and surveyed what appeared to be the former living room. The Sterns had lived there for decades, but within hours their home had been torn apart and almost every item carted away: the tables, chairs, even the curtains had been stolen.

Noike walked over to the large window that faced the Great Synagogue, the largest prayer house in Luboml. The synagogue was made of whitewashed brick and decorated with a fortress-style roof, exactly like the big synagogue in Maciejow. German officers and Ukrainian police were lining Jews up and pushing them through the synagogue archway. Noike thought he was far enough away that no one would notice him, but one of the Ukrainian officers must have seen his shadow. The officer finished leading his prisoners into the synagogue, then turned and headed towards Noike.

"Herschel, one of the policemen at the synagogue saw me in the window—he's coming towards us now!"

The boys dashed back up to the attic, closed the little door, and sat on top of it.

Moments later, they heard the officer enter the house, ascend the stairs to the main floor, then go room-to-room searching for the shadow he had seen in the window. He paused below the attic entrance before climbing the long, narrow ladder. The boys could hear the ladder creak and groan as the officer stepped on each rung. They pressed their hands and feet deep into the attic door, pushing their hands into the beam supporting the ceiling.

They were quiet, dead quiet. They would not give themselves up.

The policeman pushed against the door but it would not budge. He pushed again, this time even harder, breathing heavily and grunting as he tried to force the door open. He was probably strong enough, but the ladder was steep and unsteady, making it difficult for him to put all of his weight into the door.

"*Holera!*" the policeman cursed with frustration. He climbed back down and returned to his work at the synagogue.

The boys collapsed onto the attic floor and stared at the ceiling. They heard voices coming from the small space between the two houses. Ukrainian policemen were ordering a group of Jews to stand against the house while they searched them for valuables. Many people were crying but one voice stood out from the others.

"Mother, mother, are they going to shoot us?" a little girl asked in Yiddish.

Noike recognized the voice as Rachel, a young cousin who had been hiding in the bedroom next door. She was eight years old; her brother, Shmuel, who was also standing against the house, was six. Their mother tried to calm them but their fate was unmistakable—the police, the rifles, the screaming in the streets. As Noike imagined the group being led to their deaths, he felt dead himself: another mass grave awaited him.

The graves were in a wooded area in the outskirts of town, less than three miles away. Jewish men had been forced to dig the graves several months earlier, convinced that the massive pit was for a pottery factory. Jews had been doing all kinds of hard labor from the beginning of the occupation; few suspected that the Germans had different plans for the pit.

Noike and Herschel stayed in the attic the rest of the afternoon, their bodies anchored to the floor. Death was prowling all around them, swallowing men, women, girls, boys, babies. There seemed to be no way to escape its reach. If they dared to venture outside, they would be captured; if they managed to stay hidden they would eventually die of hunger or thirst. The boys remained quiet and motionless, uncertain how to save themselves.

Eventually the boys went over to the window and observed an elderly man, holding what seemed to be his grandchildren's hands, walking from the synagogue to the graves. He had a long, white beard and wore a dark suit with *tzitzis*; the fringe fluttered in the light autumn wind. The children were neatly dressed and well behaved, as if it were a special occasion; they were unaware of the atrocities that awaited them. The grandfather and other adults also walked passively, silently, down the main street. They knew they would soon be killed; no one wanted any additional suffering.

Their cousin Hanna was also captured that day but she refused to go in silence.

As the SS and the Ukrainian police were rounding up a group of Jews, they tried to alleviate the mass hysteria that had ensued, tried to make their jobs easier: "We are not going to kill you; we are sending you to work in a brick factory," the officers had said. Hanna, who was part of the roundup and knew differently, yelled: "Don't believe them—they want to kill all of us!" One of the SS officers walked up to Hanna, placed his gun inside her mouth, and fired.

In the early evening Noike and Herschel heard a young woman whispering in Yiddish near the attic entrance. They could not make out what she was saying, having moved several feet away from the door and into a dark corner where the roof sloped down. "Hello," they said in hushed Yiddish. "Is someone over there?"

"*Ich bin Yiddish*," she replied, walking towards them. Calling oneself *Yiddish*, the Yiddish word for "Jew", was one of the ways Jews would identify themselves as allies in situations like this one.

When the woman was within a few inches, they realized it was their cousin Esther, one of their uncle Falik's three daughters. She was about twenty-years-old with an oval face, almond-colored eyes, and wavy, chin-length hair; she was known as a leader among her peers. Esther was checking all of the hiding places in her house and the neighboring one, searching for friends and relatives who had survived the raids. She had also been hiding next door, in a small room on the third floor.

"You managed to get away!" she said, shocked to see her cousins, knowing that their hiding place had been captured.

"Where are your sisters?" Herschel asked.

"They are fine, thank God. Sabina and Fania are also safe—they didn't find our hiding place. We're planning to leave Luboml tonight and walk to Vladimir Volynski, a Jewish ghetto about thirty miles away. If you want to come, meet us next door in one hour, on the stairs to the third floor."

"We'll meet you there," Herschel said, before Esther walked back into the darkness.

"I'm going to look for food next door," Noike said. Several bundles of dried food had been brought into the room, but they had been there for less than one day.

"You're not going anywhere," Herschel told Noike. "I'll go get food and you'll stay here."

*Why do I have to stay behind while Herschel goes out?*

Noike used to tag along with Herschel and his friends less than a year ago. But things were different now: he had learned how to take care of himself, how to do things on his own. After Herschel left he crawled back through the broken tiles and headed next door. He made his way down to the basement, where Falik had run his carbonated soda business.

Looking at the bottles of fruit juice lining the shelves Noike was reminded of a trip he took with Falik to a nearby lake in the dead of winter. He had stood on the frozen grass, bundled in his wool hat, scarf, and mittens, watching as the men cut large blocks of ice and loaded them onto the sleigh. Noike thought of Falik and his other uncles wondering if they had made it safely to the bunker in the woods.

Scanning the cellar walls, Noike spotted two teenage boys huddled on the floor, near some cases of empty soda bottles. He had never seen the boys before but he was certain they were Jews who had escaped from another part of the neighborhood. Noike nodded at them but they did not exchange words.

Noike was about to take some of the concentrated cherry and strawberry juices when he heard the sound of heavy boots nearby and someone shouting "*Raus, raus!* Out, out!" He wanted to leave through the side door but he was afraid he would run into the police. There was a small window but it was too high for him to reach.

"Can you help me through the window?" he asked the teenage boys.

"Someone might see us if we go near the window," one said, refusing to help.

"Please, I need to find my brother," he begged again.

The boys hesitated, then finally agreed. Hoisting him by his legs, they lifted Noike up into air and pushed him through the window. As he landed on the ground again he heard the Germans shouting, "*Raus, raus!*" from next door.

Fearing the Germans would capture him if he returned to the house next door, he sprinted up the stairs to meet his young relatives. When he reached the second floor landing, he found his three cousins, two aunts, and two boys about to leave for Vladimir Volynski. He thought one of the boys was Herschel but soon realized it was Leibel, one of Esther's maternal cousins. The other boy was Isaac, the young man Noike met when he first arrived in Luboml. Herschel was not there.

"Did Herschel come earlier?" Noike asked with a worried look.

"No," Esther answered. "We've been waiting near the stairs for more than an hour. We need to leave now—they are double checking many of the homes."

Noike immediately imagined the worst: Herschel captured; Herschel held in the synagogue; Herschel shot in the mass graves. *No, this can't be happening!* They had made it through the worst; they had promised never to leave each other. But maybe he escaped from the police again, maybe he was hiding in another house in Luboml, maybe he would meet them in Vladimir Volynski.

"Noike," Esther grabbed his shoulders. "Noike we have to leave now. If Herschel made it to safety, he'll find us in Vladimir Volynski."

# 13

## LOST CEMETERIES
*New York. circa 1980*

"Would you like to visit your grandfather with *Baba* and I?" my mother asked when I was eleven. "We are going to the cemetery on Sunday; it's on Staten Island." *Baba* is the Yiddish term for grandmother; this *Baba* was my maternal grandmother.

"Yes, I want to go," I said, nodding my head. I had looked at his photo for years, but now I could finally see where he rested every day, every night.

That Sunday we picked up my grandmother in the Bronx.

"Hello, *mamela*," she said when she got into the car, wearing one of her signature polyester dress suits and carrying her purse with the big snap.

"Hi *Baba*," I said, leaning over the front seat to give her a kiss.

She had had a difficult life, losing most of her family during the war, then losing her husband to a tragic accident two decades later. Although she didn't have much money, she insisted on sending her grandchildren twenty dollars for every birthday. But more than money, we loved her homemade *pierogi*, *knishes*, and cinnamon rolls.

We parked the car on the road outside the cemetery and meandered through its "neighborhoods" and "streets." Standing over my grandfather's grave I felt relief more than sadness—he had a place: Rymalower section G, plot #30.

Why couldn't we visit my father's mother, father, sister, and brother at a cemetery? Europe was far away, I understood, but we never visited them. Not seeing their resting place led me to believe that they might still be alive, in Europe, waiting for us to call.

Every year when the new telephone books arrived I would thumb through the White Pages, looking up all of the Ginsburgs and where they lived. "Dad, do you know Henry Ginsburg who lives in New City, N.Y.?" I once asked my father, secretly hoping that Herschel had come to the United States and had anglicized his name.

"No, pussycat, I don't," he replied.

"How about Harold Ginsburg in Suffern, N.Y.?" I asked, knowing that the anglicized version of Herschel could have many variations. "Maybe we're related to him?"

"I don't think so. Ginsburg is a common name."

Disappointed, I would slam the book shut, stuffing it in the kitchen cabinet with all of the White Pages from previous years. My father never had the heart to tell me to stop looking, so I continued to search, flipping through the White Pages whenever we went to a new town, whenever the new edition showed up the following year.

A trip to the beach when I was still in junior high led me to press my father on the subject once again. Returning from a dip in the ocean I found him sitting by the pool, talking to another guest at the hotel.

I stepped into the shallow end and began swimming the pool's perimeter, practicing the strokes I had learned at day camp: breast stroke, crawl stroke, side stroke. As I swam past my father and the woman I could make out parts of their conversation.

"No, they were all killed," he told the woman.

I instantly knew he was talking about his family in Europe, saying things that I had heard from other adults, but never my father. I had often heard him strike up similar conversations with strangers, but he never mentioned the subject with his own family.

I circled back to the deep end as the woman stood up to leave.

I swam up to my father, his feet still dangling in the water.

"How do you know your family isn't still alive?" I asked.

He looked up, not realizing that I had been within earshot of the conversation and uncertain how to answer my question.

"I just know," he said with effort.

"But maybe they're still in Europe and they just don't know you're here."

"No, baby, I just know," he repeated, ending the conversation abruptly.

How did he know? I wanted to ask again. I had seen dozens of reunions on television dramas and talk shows—adopted daughters found their birth mothers; twin sisters separated at birth met when they turned eighteen; half brothers learned about half sisters later in life. If it could happen to them, why not us?

I had imagined the reunion countless times, countless ways. In one fantasy, my family and I would be sitting in the kitchen, watching television, when the phone would ring. Leaping out of my seat, I would lunge for the phone.

"Hello, Ginsburg residence," I would say, in my most grown-up voice.

The voice on the other end would sound like my father's, revealing slight traces of an Eastern European accent: "May I speak to Leon Ginsburg?"

"Dad, it's for you!" I would tell him as I handed the phone over, unwinding the mustard yellow cord so it could reach across the table to my father.

"Noikele, it's Herschel, your brother. Momma, Blimele, and I have been trying to find you for years but you changed your first name, and now you spell Ginzburg with an 's', not a 'z'."

My father would be overcome with emotion, a relief and joy he had not felt in over thirty years. Tears would run down his face and onto his shirt and pants, until he was drenched. My mother, brother, sister and I would all look at each other, instantly knowing that the miraculous reunion would finally happen, that we would all be together.

"See," I would tell my father, "You didn't have enough hope!"

It was that simple.

Their first meeting would land, fortuitously, on my birthday. Standing in front of my birthday cake, the candles would twinkle, lighting up the faces of my long lost grandmother, aunt, uncle, and newfound cousins standing around the table. They would wear birthday hats and sing Happy Birthday, then urge me to blow out the candles before they melted, before I could no longer make my wish.

"Wait a moment," my father would say, stepping back to take a photo.

The flash would make everyone blink and rub their eyes.

"Make your wish, make your wish," they would say in a chorus.

"But I already have my wish," I would reply.

Years later, when I finally learned what had happened to my father's family, I understood why he never promised the miraculous reunion. Maybe he had the same dreams at one time, but years passed, and the dreams never materialized. Maybe he realized that not knowing is sometimes better. As a child, not knowing gave me hope. Year after year, I would blow out my birthday candles, wishing my long lost relatives would come next year.

## 14

# WHERE IS THE SIXTH ONE?
### Luboml to Olesk, Poland. October 1942

The eight young survivors quietly made their way down the stairs to the alley between Falik's house and the neighboring one. Many of them carried small bundles containing *sucharky*–dried bread—and other food that would keep for several days. Isaac and Esther, the natural leaders, were the first ones to enter the alley. Noike and the others walked behind them, in single file or pairs.

While snaking through the alley they passed a dead body that someone had covered with a blanket, a final gesture of dignity for the poor soul. Bluma nearly fainted when she saw the blood stains. She was nineteen years old, the youngest and most sensitive of Falik's three daughters. She held hands with her older sister, Faige, who tried to calm Bluma despite her own terror, reminding her that they still had each other.

There was no full moon and lights no longer glowed in the empty Jewish homes. As the group approached the edge of town, their surroundings grew darker and darker, until everything around them turned pitch black. All at once they melted into the night. They created a human chain, holding onto another arm, shoulder, or hand to stay connected.

Noike searched for Isaac and grabbed his hand. It felt warm, strong, safe.

Isaac squeezed Noike's hand tightly as if to say, "Don't worry, I've got you, I won't let go."

They soon reached the railroad tracks, the same ones Noike followed when he walked from the village of Bilitch to Luboml. Across the tracks, a group of German soldiers were shooting flares, lighting up the sky to catch anyone who tried to leave Luboml. Most of the people in town would not make it past them: escapees were shot on sight.

The group stood in a row of bushes several feet from the tracks, watching the flares go up one after the other. During a brief pause between each flare the sky would turn an ashen gray and then darken once again. Isaac spotted a shed beside the tracks and suggested that they run for cover there between the flares. They held their bundles close to their chests and readied themselves for the run.

The next flare shot up into the sky, lighting up their surroundings and giving them a last good look at the place they had once called home. As the light from the flare dimmed, the group bolted for the shed, flattening their bodies against its thick, splintering wood. After the next flare went up, they ran across the tracks, through the freshly cut fields and into the forest.

Once they were deep in the woods, Sabina and Fania separated from the group and headed towards Maciejow in search of their younger sister, Hanka. They prayed the falsified papers they were carrying—documents that identified them as Polish Catholics—would get them to Kovel, a big town where no one would recognize them. It would be easier for the women to assume a different identity: their bodies would not reveal their faith. Men and boys, who were circumcised at birth, could not hide their Jewishness.

Now they were six.

THE GROUP HAD BEEN WALKING FOR SEVERAL MILES when they heard the sound of running water just beyond their path. They lay down on the ground to drink the water, not caring if it was dirty or tasted of weeds and grass. Feeling refreshed from the cool drink, they forged ahead through the woods. As Noike stepped over the logs and pushed low-hanging branches out of his way, he recalled the Jewish holiday of *Tu Bishvat*, when his family and many other Jews would go into the woods to celebrate nature, planting new trees and blessing the ones that grew in abundance. One of the festival songs found its way into his head:

> *Come outside o come with me,*
> *In my hand I hold a tree.*
> *Let us plant it, it will be*
> *A good friend to you and me...*

In the darkness a Ukrainian cemetery emerged; the sight of it returned Noike to the present. The cemetery was relatively large and bordered by a low cement wall. Peering over the wall, the group scanned the sea of headstones;

most were crowned with the Ukrainian Orthodox cross and engraved with epitaphs in Cyrillic. Some of the graves had been visited recently—the leaves on the floral wreaths were still green. Noike thought back to Maciejow and Luboml, thought back to all of the people who had been denied a proper resting place. Would anyone be left to visit them one day? Who would come to say a *kaddish*, to leave a stone?

The group sat down and leaned against the cemetery wall to rest for a short time. Faige and Bluma unpacked some of the *sucharky* and passed them around. Isaac, Laibel, and Esther discussed their route, considering which towns to avoid and which parts of the woods were safe. Noike was still exhausted from the journey from Maciejow. He leaned his head back and immediately drifted off to sleep.

One, maybe two hours passed.

Noike opened his eyes: it was pitch black, still the middle of the night. Moving his hands along the cool cement wall, he inched towards the place where his cousins had been sitting. Silence. He crawled further along the wall, whispering their names. He guessed that they had moved into the cemetery for shelter, but he was reluctant to follow them inside. He had always been afraid of cemeteries.

Jewish children were not supposed to visit cemeteries before they reached *Bar Mitzvah*, their thirteenth birthday. Noike once overheard his grandfather talking to Herschel about their father's *Yahrtzeit*, the anniversary of his death. "When you turn thirteen, it will be time for you to visit your *Tate* and say the *kaddish* in his honor," Yakob said, patting Herschel on the back. Yakob never imagined that Herschel might not reach his thirteenth birthday.

Noike looked over the cemetery wall and softly called, "Isaac, Isaac, Isaac..."

No answer.

The sounds of nature grew louder. Giant trees twisted with rage in the wind, thrashing their branches like giant scarecrows. Unknown creatures rustled through the dry fall leaves. Noike wondered if the group had been taken away by cemetery ghosts—spirits angered by strangers violating their resting place. The longer he stayed outside the cemetery, the more his mind played tricks on him. Finally, he summoned the courage to climb into the cemetery.

He looked behind dozens of tombstones but found no one.

Deeper into the cemetery his eyes were drawn to a mausoleum surrounded by tall shrubs and a linked, chain fence. The deceased must have been someone rich or famous, for his tomb was the largest one on the grounds. Noike thought his cousins might be hiding behind the shrubs. He inched towards the mausoleum and called again, "Isaac, Isaac, Isaac…"

Still no answer.

He jumped back over the cemetery wall and noticed a cluster of boxed shadows surrounded by a small grove of pine trees across the way. As he walked towards the shadows, a thatched farmhouse with painted trim came into view. Several yards away from the house there stood a row of three wooden barns, grayish brown from decades of wear.

He walked over to the first barn and pulled the handle—it was locked. The second barn door swung open with a gentle tug but the stall was filled with several smelly pigs, grunting and squealing as they jostled for room in the tight space. He was about to give up and leave the farm when he tried the third barn door. It was open and in the far corner lay a black and white Holstein cow, fast asleep.

A cow is a nice, friendly animal, Noike thought as he walked towards her and gently stroked her bristly white fur. The cow remained still, unaware of the little boy beside her, unaware of the refuge she would provide him for the night. He lay down next to the creature and soon fell asleep to the rhythm of her warm breaths.

Noike woke up before dawn and surveyed his surroundings. The barn was empty aside from the sleeping cow, a couple of metal buckets, and a hayloft crammed with bales of hay. Knowing that farmers milk their cows first thing in the morning, he decided to move into the hayloft. With no ladder in sight, he took a running leap from the back of the barn, caught the edge of the loft floor and hoisted himself into the soft bundles of hay.

The pull-up bar at home must have paid off.

When the Russian army occupied Maciejow, the troops often staged military exercises in the center of town. The young boys, impressed by the soldiers, started doing calisthenics at home and racing each other at school. Around this time, Noike and his brother installed a smooth metal pull-up bar in the back of their house. Herschel would help Noike up and count each time his chin extended over the bar.

Noike thought of Herschel and wondered where he was at that moment: Luboml, Vladimir Volynski, the woods? He also thought of his cousins: Had they been captured while he slept? Had they left without him? Why was he suddenly all alone?

A couple of hours later, he heard the barn door open, then some soft footsteps. Peeking over the bales of hay, he watched a young woman grab one of the metal buckets against the wall and approach the cow. Her wispy, dark hair was covered in a kerchief, and she wore a long, white apron with knee-high work boots. Thinking it was best to get her attention while they were alone, Noike cupped his hand over his mouth and gently coughed.

The woman was startled but seemed relieved that it was just a little boy.

"Don't be afraid," he said in Ukrainian, "I'm just lost—I promise to leave soon."

"Wait until the shepherd comes and takes the cow out," she whispered, walking towards the edge of the loft. "He should be here within the hour. You want something to eat?"

"Thank you, *Pani*," Noike said, nodding his head.

The woman soon returned with a freshly baked *boolke*, a small roll, and a cup of milk. "Remember, don't come down until the shepherd has left," she said, before closing the barn door.

While lying in the loft Noike heard horse carts rattling down the road in front of the farm. Two drivers stopped and started talking about "Jews hiding in the graveyard with dollars." Noike knew that his cousins had received dollars from their relatives living in the United States. He was about to head back to the cemetery to warn them when he heard the shepherd entering the barn.

"Come on, girl," the shepherd, a blonde boy of about twelve, said as he put a rope around the cow's neck. He gently tugged the cow into the yard and kicked the barn door shut.

Noike waited a little while, then climbed down and looked into the farmyard: chicken and geese were running loose in the yard but the shepherd and other farmers were long gone. He crossed the road and headed back to the cemetery. In the bright morning sun he could easily find where his cousins had stopped the night before; he began searching for them from there.

Again, he called, "Isaac, Isaac, Isaac…"

"Shhh…" a voice whispered. He walked towards the voice and found the group crouched inside a row of bushes along the cemetery wall, camouflaged with large leafy branches pulled from the nearby trees. Isaac and Laibel moved some branches aside and helped Noike into the bushes.

"I heard Ukrainians talking about Jews with dollars in the cemetery," Noike rushed to tell them.

"Were they policemen?" Faige shuddered, terrified of the men. "Esther, we should leave—we don't have much protection in these bushes."

"No, we can't leave now," Esther said firmly. "We can gather more branches to improve our cover but we can't get on the road until dark."

Although the group feared capture in the cemetery, it was even more dangerous to travel during the day. With the open fields and empty country roads, they could be spotted less than a half mile away, easy targets for anyone willing to capture them and turn them over to the police.

After sunset they began walking again, alternating between the woods and the road to Vladimir Volynski. They walked most of the night, stopping to rest in a heavily wooded area. Faige passed around small pieces of the *sucharky* then lay down with Bluma. Everyone took turns napping to build energy for the long journey ahead.

It could not have been more than an hour when Noike opened his eyes and discovered that a layer of dew had settled on his pants. When they stood up to leave, he asked everyone to wait: "I can't move—my pants are frozen," he said, trying to bend them back into shape. Every moment was life or death for the group, yet they all had to stop and laugh at the amusing sight of Noike in his frozen pants.

As they continued their journey, Bluma began talking about the hiding place that her brother Yankel and other Jews from the lumber brigade had built in the woods. None of the girls had actually been there, but they knew it was behind the nearby village of Polap and could hold at least thirty people.

"I'll go and find it," Noike volunteered. He wanted to impress his older cousins, show them that he could be brave and resourceful even though he was younger than all of them. He also wondered if Herschel might have escaped to Polap.

"Have you ever been to Polap?" Bluma asked. "You have to go through the woods, back the way we came."

"The woods are vast, Noike," Esther said. "Are you sure you want to go?"

"Sure, I can find it," he said brazenly as he ran off.

Noike started walking through the woods back towards Luboml. He had covered a couple of miles, weaving through the tall pine trees while keeping his eyes on the edge of the woods, when he spotted a cluster of ripe blueberry bushes. His eyes glistened with pleasure; he was starving from the long walk through the woods.

Crouching down, he went from bush to bush, popping berries into his mouth and stuffing some in his pockets for later. When he had collected enough berries, he stood up and realized that he had lost his orientation. He couldn't figure out which direction would take him to Vladimir Volynski and which pointed back to Luboml.

*The woods are vast, Noike.*

Suddenly, he heard gunshots in the distance. Turning towards the source of the shots, he came face-to-face with a man carrying an axe in one hand. His sleeves were rolled up to his elbows; the front of his shirt was dusted with specks of leaves and dirt. He appeared to be looking for firewood.

"*Dobry vecchir,*" Noike greeted the man in Ukrainian.

The man nodded at Noike and set his axe down.

"Can you tell me how to go to Vladimir Volynski?" Noike asked.

"You'll want to head in that direction," the man replied in Polish as he pointed to the road heading south, then added: "You should get out of the area as soon as you can—the Germans and the Ukrainian police are still hunting Jews."

Though many Poles celebrated when their towns were declared "Jew free," some would go to great lengths to protect Jews. Sometimes their motivations were complex but often the Poles were moved simply by the desire to help their friend or fellow man. There were not enough of these good people in Poland: it is widely agreed that local collaboration enabled the massive genocide.

Noike left the woods immediately and headed back to the road. This time he mentally noted every turn and natural landmark: the abandoned barn, the picket fence, the fallen tree trunk. Golden haystacks and lush, green pastures began to spring up on either side of the road. Most of the pastures were empty, except for one where two Ukrainian farm boys, ragged and barefoot, were talking to each other as they watched over their cows. They were about the same age as Noike.

"*Zyd, Zyd!*" they yelled at Noike. "Jew! Jew! Give us your hat!"

The hat had belonged to a neighbor of Falik's who had been in Red Army and fled to Russia when Germany attacked. It was made of wool and had earflaps that could be tied down under your chin; the top was crowned with a little red ball. The thick, sturdy material helped keep him warm at night.

The boys continued to shout in Ukrainian: "Give us your hat!" They started to tie up the cows, determined to get the little prize.

Noike ran for the woods as he loosened the string under his chin, pulled the hat off, and threw it deep into the pastures. The little ball seemed to steer and propel the hat forward as it sailed into the tall grasses.

The boys kicked and pushed each other, screaming, "It's mine! It's mine!"

Noike ran madly into the woods, tripping over tree roots, running into low-hanging branches. Safely hidden in the dense forest cover, he leaned against a tree and paused to catch his breath. The faint sound of the boys, still fighting over his hat, could be heard in the distance, then silence. A flock of birds flew overhead, gently rustling the giant oak and birch trees, sending a few leaves drifting down from the canopy. Worried that the boys might come looking for him, Noike stayed in the woods as he walked back to his cousins. He emerged when he reached an empty stretch of the road not far from their resting place. He spotted his fellow travelers walking several yards ahead.

"Hey, you left me!" Noike said when he caught up with them.

"Noike, you were gone for almost two hours," Esther said defensively. "We assumed you had been caught!"

Noike was hurt that they had left without him but he had grown to understand the ever-changing rules of survival. Most Jews would never return from a risky journey into the woods; waiting longer for him would only put their lives at risk.

The group continued walking south, toward the village of Olesk, another Ukrainian nationalistic stronghold about the same size as Bilitch. Nearly all of the villagers were engaged in agriculture; few were educated beyond primary school.

"We need to get some more food," Esther said when they stopped to rest. They concealed themselves inside a tangle of bushes near a stream.

"Noike, do you want to try and find something nearby?" Isaac asked, thinking someone younger was less likely to get captured by the locals.

"Sure, I'll go," Noike agreed, his adrenaline still flowing from the recent chase.

Isaac handed him several small packets of saccharin, a rare commodity, to trade in exchange for food.

"I'll meet you back here once I find something," Noike said.

"Don't stay away so long this time," Esther reminded him.

Noike had been walking for about a mile when he spotted a farmhouse with smoke streaming from one corner of the yard. He made his way towards the smoke and discovered a *parovnik*, a kettle used for steaming food. The *parovnik* had three parts: the wood burner at the bottom, the tray for water in the middle, and the container for the food at the top. This one was filled with potatoes.

As he was eying the potatoes a burly Ukrainian farmer dressed in flannel and work pants came out of the house.

"What are you looking for?" The farmer's eyes narrowed.

"Can I have some food, sir?" Noike asked, stepping away from the *parovnik*.

"Sorry," he said, lifting the lid to check on the potatoes, "I don't have anything to give you."

The Germans threatened to severely punish anyone who assisted Jews. Giving potatoes to a hungry Jewish boy was cause for a brutal beating or worse.

"Can I trade this saccharin for the potatoes?" Noike asked, pulling two packets from his pocket.

The man eyed the saccharin. "You can have some, but they're not ready," he said, snatching the saccharin packets out of Noike's hand. "It will be at least another fifteen or twenty minutes."

"I'll wait for them," Noike said, sitting down near the warm *parovnik*, concealed from the road.

The farmer went back into his house and shut the door.

With each passing minute, the smell of the cooked potatoes grew stronger and stronger. Noike imagined taking his first bite, the warm chunks steaming inside his mouth, crumbling into tiny pieces.

The farmer returned when the potatoes were done and pulled two from the steamer. He handed them to Noike, who stuffed them inside his coat pockets. The hot treat warmed his hands and stomach.

"*Pan*, I need four more," Noike said.

"I need to feed these to the pigs this afternoon," the farmer sighed, annoyed that he might have to make another batch.

Noike reached into his pocket and offered him the rest of the saccharin.

"All right, all right, but I can't give you any more than that." He pulled four more potatoes out of the steamer and grudgingly handed them to Noike.

The group was shocked when Noike returned bearing hot potatoes; they were even more pleased when they realized there were enough for everyone to have their own. They ate with great hunger, burning the roofs of their mouths as they devoured their first warm meal in days.

Later that evening Esther and Noike set out to find more food for the walk to Vladimir Volynski. They were running out of the *sucharky*, yet they still had almost twenty miles left in the journey. The two of them crawled out of the bushes and headed for the road, searching for farmhouses with kerosene lamps glowing in the windows. The road was dark and empty; most of the farmers must have already gone to bed.

Without warning they found themselves within a few feet of a young man who was not much taller than Esther. He was wearing a Ukrainian police uniform under his coat and his eyes were glassy—he must have been walking home from the local pub.

"Where do you think you're going?" he slurred.

"We're going to meet some friends," Esther explained in Ukrainian. Her experience with the family business had helped to perfect her language skills; many of their customers had been Ukrainian.

"I'm with the police department." The officer pulled back his coat, revealing the badge on his uniform. "You know, I could arrest both of you for being out past curfew."

Esther and Noike kept silent.

"But, if you want to come with me for a while," he trailed off, looking greedily at Esther.

Noike started hanging onto Esther, acting like her baby brother, tugging hard at her coat sleeve. Although he was acting like a child on the outside, the growing man inside him was ready to attack. He noticed that the officer was unarmed and became convinced that the two of them could tackle him if he tried anything.

"He doesn't have a weapon," Noike whispered to Esther in Yiddish.

"I would go with you, but I have my little brother here," she then said, stroking Noike's head. "But I can bring him back to my sister and meet you later."

"Well, I need to get back home now," the officer said, less interested in the rendez-vous. "But maybe I'll see you later."

Esther and Noike walked in silence as they continued down the road, tightly gripping each other's hands. In the distance, they spotted a faint light coming from a thatched farmhouse that was set back from the road and surrounded by a patchwork of vegetable and flower gardens. They made their way towards the entrance and knocked on the door. An old Ukrainian farmer with a pot belly and thick gray hair soon appeared in the doorway.

"*Dobry vecchir*," Esther greeted the man in Ukrainian.

"*Dobry vecchir*," he replied, buttoning his sweater and straightening his hair. "What can I do for you?"

"We are terribly sorry to disturb you this time of night," Esther said. "Can we trouble you for something to eat?"

"Well, I don't have much, but I can give you some vegetables," he said, waving both of them into the house. The inside of his home was simple: a bed stood in one corner, a rough wooden table and chair were in the center of the room, a black stove was against the wall. He appeared to live alone.

The old man lumbered slowly down to the cellar, his body swaying left and right with each step down the narrow wooden stairs. They heard him moving, opening, shutting crates. He returned with a bunch of carrots and a few beets covered in a thin layer of dirt.

"You can sleep here if you like, but I only have one bed," he said, motioning to the narrow bed in the corner. Clumps of straw poked through the worn corners of the mattress; a gray, wool blanket lay folded at one end.

"*Diakuyu tobi*," Esther thanked him, but declined. Although the man seemed kind and sleeping in a bed of any kind was inviting, they did not want to risk capture or separate from the group. "We appreciate the vegetables you gave us," she added.

When Noike and Esther returned to the stream the group resumed their journey, taking advantage of the protection afforded by the cover of night. The country road was dark and silent, except for a gentle wind blowing through the trees and the rustle of crisp fall leaves. Tired from his adventure into the woods, Noike started to lag behind after a couple of hours. He was about to run ahead and suggest that they stop for a break when the squeak of wheels and the *clop clop* of horseshoes broke the night silence. Everyone moved off the road, into the narrow ditch that separated the road from the fields below.

They lied with their faces close to the ground; the cold earth was chilling.

Within a couple of minutes a farmer on a horse and wagon drifted past them, then faded back into the darkness. They remained motionless until they could no longer hear the horse's footsteps. After resuming their journey they walked no more than a few yards before they heard more horseshoes coming from the village of Olesk. Again the group moved off the road before anyone could see them. Noike, who was still lagging behind, lay in a ditch about fifty feet away. When he looked up he saw a man pass by on a horse and saddle, scanning both sides of the road.

As Noike lay there, waiting to see what the group would do next, he heard a humming noise coming from the direction of the village. Craning his neck above the edge of the ditch, he caught a glimpse of a Ukrainian police officer riding a bicycle with a rifle strapped over his shoulder. The officer stopped a few feet past Noike, raised his gun, and fired one shot in the air.

"*Vilezai*! Get out!" he yelled in Ukrainian.

Noike abandoned his bundles and started crawling away from the police, towards a storm pipe that ran under the road. He heard screams as the police fired their guns and chased the others into the fields. Within minutes, more police on bicycles surrounded the area, carrying flashlights and lanterns.

"Watch the fire!" the new arrivals yelled, afraid they might accidentally shoot one another in the darkness.

Noike hunched over and continued running towards the storm pipe. One of the men must have heard or seen his movement: gunshots flew in his direction, grazing the inside of his left foot as he dove inside the pipe. He crawled further inside and stopped to catch his breath. Reaching down for his foot, he pressed his pant leg against his wound, trying to alleviate the sharp pain.

"Where is the sixth one?" one of the men yelled in Ukrainian. They had captured all of the others and were now looking for him.

Noike pulled himself through the storm pipe and stopped in the middle, where the road curved. Underground he heard footsteps approach the opening of the storm pipe, then stop. Beams of light bounced off the inside of the pipe as one of the officers panned his flashlight back and forth. Noike covered his head, imagining a tide of bullets flooding the pipe and the police dragging his limp body out into the street.

But the light from the flashlight grew dimmer; the man walked away.

Noike remained still as the police interrogated the group further down the road. Muffled voices could be heard as they searched his cousins and tore open their remaining bundles of *sucharky* and other things. Sometime later he heard their footsteps pass overhead as he lay there, shaking.

# 15

# LITTLE BOY IN A HAYSTACK
*Olesk, Poland. October 1942*

Noike remained for some time in the underground storm pipe, entombed within its thick cement walls. He was afraid one of the policemen might be standing outside, waiting for him to surface from his hiding place. Cool gusts of air rushed through the pipe, chilling his entire body. He curled himself into a tight ball, tried not to let his teeth chatter. Even if the police had left, he feared they would return to the scene of the crime, determined to find the one that got away.

*Where is the sixth one?*

Noike tried to stay awake, to be prepared should they return, but at some point his overwhelmed body slipped into sleep. An hour or two later, a rooster from a nearby farm crowed in the darkness. Noike scrambled to one end of the pipe, listening for signs of the police, but it was silent. Peeking his head out into the darkness, he was relieved to discover that the road was deserted and it was not yet morning.

He pulled himself out of the pipe and stretched his limbs. As he started to walk down the road, he was reminded of the wound in his foot; the burning sensation pulsed with every step. When he reached the spot where his cousins had been rounded up, the pain in his foot receded, replaced with flashbacks to the night before: the wagon, the man on horseback, the men on bicycles. He surveyed the detritus left in the wake of their capture: bits of the *sucharky*, the wrapping from their packages, torn clothing.

Noike imagined his cousins standing there, pleading with the police to take whatever they wanted and let them go. It looked as if they had searched everything piece by piece, taking the best loot for themselves before heading back to the police station in town. They had hit the jackpot: the girls had sewn diamonds into the linings of their wool coats; gold coins lined the soles of their shoes.

Noike was overwhelmed by sadness and fear: sadness because his cousins and the boys had been like sisters and brothers, taking him under their wings; fear because they were older than him, stronger than him, and yet they could not survive. He wondered where they were taken and what would happen to them. He also felt a deep sense of guilt and wondered: *Why did I escape again when others did not?*

Noike picked up some pieces of the *sucharky,* thinking he should have some on hand as he continued his journey, but then reconsidered, dropping them to the ground. He pictured the police tearing the *sucharky* packages open with their filthy hands, throwing them aside when they realized they didn't contain any hidden treasures, then lunging for his cousins' shoes and clothing. He tried to put the events out of his mind; he had to get away from that place.

Stripped of his leaders, he had no choice but to forge ahead alone.

About a mile down the road Noike came upon a series of small farms. As he was about to pass one of them, he heard low growls coming from the inside the yard. Two mangy dogs with gray hair were sitting near the barn tracking his every move. The larger of the two ran to the fence and began barking, the smaller one soon followed.

Noike stopped in his tracks, worried that the barking would wake the farm's owners. He took a few steps back, crouched behind a cluster of bushes, and waited for the dogs to retreat. The dogs ran along the fence, bobbing their heads up and down, sniffing for the intruder. Sensing that he had left, they trotted back towards the barn and lay down. Relieved yet wary, Noike got up on his tiptoes to creep past the farm.

He continued walking along the road until he reached a fork marked by a Ukrainian Orthodox cross that was decorated with long, colored ribbons: pink, blue, yellow, green. On a windy day the ribbons would sail into the sky and wind themselves around the cross but that night they were limp, lifeless. Looking up he imagined what would happen if the cross toppled over at that moment, its crushing weight and sharp edges hammering him into the ground, sealing his fate. Part of him wanted the nightmare to end at that moment, another part urged him to press forward

The right arm of the cross pointed towards the road leading to Vladimir Volynski, the left arm pointed to a path that went through the woods. Taking a deep breath and opening his eyes wide, Noike tried to jolt himself awake for the long journey to Vladimir Volynski, but his eyes begged to be closed. Even if he managed to walk partway, he knew it would be dangerous to be out on the road when daylight came.

Less than a quarter mile down the road to Vladimir Volynski, he noticed a small farm with a thatched house, a garden filled with sunflowers, and two barns set away from the house. Trying to sleep in one of the barns seemed like the best option for the night.

He tugged at the barn doors but they were both locked. A few feet away from the barns stood a giant haystack. Noike crouched at its base and pulled out a few sections of hay, making a hole big enough for him to crawl through. He squeezed into the warm nest, then put the hay back into place.

He immediately fell asleep.

A few hours later he woke with a start. The farmer's wife was cursing in a shrill Ukrainian voice: "*Suki syn*!" She had come outside to feed the animals and noticed that the haystack had been disturbed; bits and pieces of hay were sticking out of Noike's hole. She ran into one of the barns and grabbed a pitchfork, determined to chase out whatever animal had crawled inside in the middle of the night.

Peeking out between the sections of hay, Noike saw her running in his direction, armed with the pitchfork. She was wearing a wide cotton skirt that reached the ground, and had a kerchief tightly knotted under her chin. Noike pushed the sections of hay open, stretched his hand out, and wailed, "Don't be scared—I'm just a boy!"

The woman dropped the pitchfork, brought her hand to her mouth, and gasped. Before he had a chance to tell her that he would leave immediately, she dashed back into the house, frantically calling her husband's name: "Vasil! Vasil!" Noike wanted to run but it was too dangerous to be outside under the morning sun.

He sat still and waited inside the haystack.

The man named Vasil ran out of the house, fastening his suspenders with one hand, holding his coat in the other. His face was still lined with sleep and covered in stubble, as if he had just rolled out of bed.

"Boy, who are you?" he asked sternly as he approached the haystack.

"I'm Falik Ginzburg's nephew," he explained. "I've come from Luboml."

Noike hoped his family connection would make the man less angry. Many farmers in the area had dealt with Falik at some point, as he had a number of shops in town frequented by Jews and non-Jews alike. He was known as an honest man, well-respected by the farming community.

The farmer looked at the frightened little boy: white as a sheet, no harm to anyone.

"*Pan*, can I have something to eat?" Noike asked. He wanted to wait to ask for food but the hunger inside of him had suddenly become unbearable.

Shaking his head in disbelief, the farmer sent his wife back to the house for food. She returned with a hunk of bread and milk for Noike, and a bundle of straw to cover the hole in the haystack.

The farmer continued to question Noike: How did he get to Olesk? Who had he been with? Where were they now?

Noike explained how he had been walking with his cousins and two boys from Luboml the previous night when the police captured them near Olesk. He had no idea where the police had taken them.

"Where were you when this happened?" the farmer asked.

"I was hiding under the road, in the storm pipe."

The farmer and his wife glanced at each other, clearly taken aback by his story. They were well aware of the raids, but they had not met any of its victims, let alone one so young.

"I'm going to Sunday church services in a little while," he told Noike. "I'll find out what happened to them, and let you know when I get back."

"Thank you, *Pan*," Noike said, bowing his head.

"You can stay here for the rest of the day, but you have to leave tonight," the farmer replied. He went back into the house, his wife following close behind.

Noike crawled back into the haystack and slept the rest of the morning.

Later that afternoon the farmer returned from church and found Noike still nestled deep inside the haystack. Squatting close to the ground, he told Noike that he had asked around and learned what had happened to his cousins.

"They shot the two boys right away, in the woods just outside of town." He paused, checking for Noike's response.

Images of Isaac and Leibel flashed before Noike's eyes. They had been alive, walking along with him less than one day ago. He was shocked that the police had wasted so little time. He had expected the boys to still be alive, held at the police station until they could turn them over to the Germans.

"And the girls? What about my cousins?" Noike asked, chewing his lower lip in anticipation. Maybe the girls were alive, maybe they had let them go.

"The three girls were put on a wagon and taken away," he explained flatly, looking away.

Noike hoped that the girls had convinced the police to take them back to Luboml, where they had more valuables hidden in the house, but it sounded like something worse had happened to them. He had heard the adults in Maciejow and Luboml talk about women being raped—the girl whom the Commandant found attractive, his mother's best friend's daughter, the pretty girl who worked at the porcelain shop. Although he did not know exactly what "rape" meant, he understood that it was a shameful act and could be deadly. He prayed that his cousins were somehow spared.

It was still light outside, but Noike wanted to get out of the area as soon as possible. He was afraid the police might come to the farm looking for him, that they would take him into the woods and shoot him too. He remembered that his mother had a long-time customer in Podswientne, a small Polish colony on the way to Vladimir Volynski. If he could hide there for a while, he could build his strength for the rest of the journey. He asked the farmer how to get to the colony.

When the main road was clear Noike crawled out of the haystack and headed to the dirt road that bisected the woods. As he was about to enter the forest, a wagon emerged from its entrance carrying about four Ukrainian policemen with rifles slung over their shoulders; they were laughing and singing songs in unison. The German army was known to provide the police with vodka as a reward for the hard work of killing Jews. Sunday was their day off, a day of celebration.

On either side of the entrance to the woods were vast wheat fields that had been cut during the recent early fall harvest. Noike crouched near the edge of one field and picked up a stone, flipping it over in his hand. Slowly, he turned away from the group on the wagon, looked out into the field, and threw the stone as far as he could. He picked up another, then another.

Noike expected them to notice that he wasn't one of the boys from the nearby villages. If they approached him, he told himself he would run into the fields. He would run so fast that they couldn't capture him; they would have to shoot him. Capture meant torture, humiliation—a postponement of the inevitable.

He continued to toss stones, waiting for the wheels to screech to a halt, for the rifle to cock. But the group continued onward, not paying attention to the little boy on the side of the road. They must have been too drunk, or maybe they didn't think he was worth the trouble.

When the wagon turned onto the main road, Noike stood up and entered the woods. Rather than walk along the well-worn path he moved into the forest, snaking through its dense foliage. After walking a couple of miles his stomach started to rumble again. Podswientne isn't that far away, he tried to convince himself, but his stomach refused to listen. He emerged from the woods when he spotted a small house with smoke coming from the chimney.

"Excuse me, *Pani*," Noike said in Polish as he stood in the doorway. "May I have something to eat?"

The woman of the house was standing alone in front of the stove, most likely preparing dinner for her husband and children working out in the fields. "*Prosze, prosze*," she said warmly. "Please, sit down and have some soup. I just finished making a pot."

Noike sat down and thanked the woman as she placed the soup in front of him. He stared into a bowl filled with a clear broth, carrots, potatoes, and small pieces of meat that floated to the top. The meat did not look like chicken or beef; he guessed it was pork. He tried not to think of the forbidden meat as he dove in, relishing every last morsel, graciously thanking the woman on his way out.

As soon as he was back in the woods, he felt waves of nausea as he thought of his *rebbes*' teachings. "Children, you may not eat any animal that has cloven hooves," the *rebbe* had said to the Talmud class. "It's against Jewish law!" Noike's knees weakened with guilt and he dropped to the ground and threw up the precious meal. The savory taste of the soup was replaced with a hot, punishing, bitter flavor. Wiping his mouth with his sleeve, he felt more foolish than redeemed: it was uncertain when he would get another meal, let alone a warm, home-cooked one.

Noike stood up and walked some more; after several miles he reached another small farming community, one he assumed was close to Podswientne. Stepping out from the woods, he noticed a couple of small thatched-roof houses, but he did not see the road leading to Podswientne.

One of the houses had a light on.

Noike went up to the window on the side of the house and peered through a gap in the curtains: a mother and daughter were in the kitchen, talking to each other as they cleaned up after the evening meal. He stood there, observing them washing dishes: an idyllic scene once normal to him now seemed surreal.

*Why can this family carry on like normal while my family has been destroyed? What did my family do to deserve such a fate?*

He scanned the inside of the house, making sure no one else was home—no one who appeared threatening. He was mainly concerned about young men and boys, the ones most likely to turn him over to the Germans. Sensing he would be safe with these women, he went around to the front door and knocked.

"Who is it?" the woman asked in Polish. The population in this area and in Podswientne was known to be almost entirely Polish.

"Excuse me, I want to find out how to go to Podswientne," Noike replied softly through the door.

The woman opened the door partway, placing one hand on the doorjamb, the other on the doorknob. She wore her long, blonde hair in a single braid and had beautiful blue eyes. Her teenaged daughter, a mirror image of her mother, stood a few feet behind her, looking through the opening, curious about the little boy alone at their door.

"*Dobry wieczór, Pani.* I'm trying to find my way to Podswientne. Can you tell me how to get there from here?"

"Who do you know in Podswientne?" she asked. She had a warm smile and kind face; she seemed like someone he could trust.

"*Pan* Shliva," he replied.

"I see," she said, trying to ascertain the connection between Noike and Mr. Shliva. The community was relatively small, making it likely that she knew Mr. Shliva, or knew someone who knew him. "Well, Podswientne is about three miles away, and you need to cut through the woods," she paused, looking down at the little boy. "I don't think it's safe for you to travel there this time of night."

She had no idea what he had been through.

"Wait a moment," she said, pulling her daughter aside and closing the door.

The woman and her daughter soon returned with a plan.

"You can sleep in the attic tonight, but my husband must not know. He's out playing cards with some of the men—he'll probably be drunk by the time he comes home. But you'll stay up there, you musn't come down until he leaves for work in the morning. I'll come up and let you know once he has left. Do you understand?"

"Yes, *Pani*, I understand," Noike said, nodding his head. "Thank you."

The next morning the woman climbed up to the attic and told Noike that it was time to leave. He followed her down the ladder and into the kitchen, where she had put out some milk and a *boolke*. As he drank the milk, she explained how to get to Podswientne.

Noike bid the mother and daughter farewell and made his way back into the wooded area close to her house. He found the footpath that had been worn by the locals, following it for about three miles. When he emerged on the other side, he saw a narrow dirt road leading to a cluster of homes, a collective he presumed to be Podswientne.

Podswientne was a colony, which meant that the families often pooled their resources and collaborated on projects that benefited their community. There were about twelve identical homes in the colony, each containing a freshly painted white house, barn, and fenced-in area for the animals. There were no signs posted with the farmer's family names, making it impossible to figure out which house was owned by Mr. Shliva.

As Noike contemplated how to find Mr. Shliva, he noticed a young boy about his age walking in his direction. "Excuse me, can you tell me where *Pan* Shliva's house is?" Noike asked in Polish.

"It's the third farm on the left," he pointed, then continued on his way.

Noike walked up the path to Mr. Shliva's house, pushed the little white gate open, and knocked on the front door.

"Oh my God, oh my God," Mrs. Shliva said with a Czech accent as she opened the door and crossed herself. The Shlivas had always lived in Poland but were of Czech decent and spoke with subtle accents. Mrs. Shliva was a robust woman with thick dark hair that she wore in a bun.

She recognized Noike from visits to his mother's fabric store over the years and the more recent trips she had made to their home. Noike remembered the last time she came to his house, carrying a basket loaded with butter, eggs, and cheese. She wanted to trade the food for cuts of fabric–she was planning to make a dress for one of her daughters. Pesel had sorted through the bolts of fabrics in advance, picking out a few floral and checkered patterns that were suitable for a young girl.

Mrs. Shliva ushered him into the house and closed the door.

"*Pan* Shliva is out working, but he will be home within the hour," she explained nervously as Noike stood near the doorway. "*Prosze, prosze*, please sit down until he returns," she said, motioning to the kitchen table.

Noike was relieved to see a familiar face, someone who knew his family.

Mrs. Shliva offered Noike a bowl of potato soup and asked about his family. He told her everything that had happened since he went into hiding less than two weeks before: the raids in Maciejow, the raids in Luboml, the capture with his cousins in Olesk. She had heard about the massacres from other adults in the area but never from a child.

"Maybe your mother was able to escape," she said, trying to ease the suffering in his eyes. "I've heard rumors that Jews are hiding in the woods."

He remained silent, unable to return her words of hope. With each passing day, the death of his family had started to become a reality.

When Mr. Shliva returned he, too, was shocked to see the little boy alive. He folded his thick, muscular arms across his chest, shaking his head as Noike recounted everything he had experienced. The Polish Czechs were more sympathetic to the plight of their Jewish neighbors than the average Polish citizen, perhaps because they had also faced discrimination as ethnic minorities. Moreover, they were Seventh Day Adventists, known to proselytize conversion of non-Christians rather than persecute them.

"Can I hide on your farm for a little while?" Noike asked.

"You can sleep in the attic tonight, but it's too dangerous to stay any longer," Mr. Shliva explained. "The SS and the Ukrainian police have been keeping a close eye on our farm; they suspect we are helping Jews in the area."

"Thank you, *Pan* Shliva," Noike replied, trying to hide his disappointment. Mr. Shliva was his only contact in the region.

Mr. Shliva wanted to leave it at that but he worried about the young boy. He also felt some level of responsibility—Pesel had been good to them over the years.

"I'm taking the wagon to Vladimir Volynski this coming Tuesday," Mr. Shliva added, knowing that Noike had tried to walk there with his cousins. "If you want to join me, I plan to leave before daybreak."

"Yes, *Pan* Shliva, I would like go with you." Noike's face brightened. He imagined finding other Jews, maybe even Herschel.

Mr. and Mrs. Shliva led him to the attic entrance in the back of the house, passing the room that their two youngest daughters shared. One of them, Zosia, was fifteen years old; the other one, Ania, was eight. Both of them had thick, dark brown hair like their mother, which they wore in two long braids fastened with colored ribbons. The girls looked up for a moment, smiled, and returned to their game. Noike wanted to play with them but he understood that he was no longer like the other children.

"We'll knock on the door when it's safe to come down in the morning," Mrs. Shliva said, handing Noike a small pillow and quilt.

Noike climbed up the ladder and said good night.

Mr. Shliva was about to close the trap door when he paused for a minute. "Noike, in case you didn't know," he said, stroking his chin, "most of the farmers don't bother to lock their small barn doors at night."

"That's right," Mrs. Shliva confirmed, looking up at Noike. "We never lock our small barn door at night."

Noike smiled at the Shlivas, fully understanding what they were telling him.

In the days that followed, Noike walked in the woods in the daylight hours, then slipped through the Shliva's small barn door after sundown. He would sleep in a dark corner of the hayloft, surrounded by bales of hay. When he heard the roosters crow in the morning, he would climb down the ladder and head back into the woods.

He had to be alert at all times, constantly looking in every direction, listening to every sound. In the woods even the smallest sound carried far, making noises that were yards away seem as if they were right behind him.

Other times, the quiet of the woods seemed to make him invisible, allowing him to travel long distances without making a sound.

One morning he was sitting in the sun near the edge of the woods, trying to get warm. Two people emerged from the forest, carrying a tree stump they had harvested. Upon seeing him, they turned back into the woods, perhaps thinking he worked for the park ranger who policed illegal foresting. When they reemerged and got a better look at him the woman said, "*To ten zydek!* It's that little Jew!" recognizing Noike from the colony. The two of them went back into the woods and collected their stump.

Aside from that encounter, Noike rarely saw anyone else around the woods, but he often heard animals. He started carrying a stick and devising escape routes in case any wild animals approached. If he needed to climb a tree he figured out a way to use his belt for leverage: first remove the belt, then close the buckle and put your feet through the loop. Hugging the tree, Noike would pull his feet up onto the trunk, using the belt to steady himself, freeing his hands to edge up the tree inch-by-inch.

One morning, as he was about to walk back into the woods, Noike spotted a yellow fox standing in the middle of the road. The fox froze and watched Noike warily, uncertain whether to continue on his path, or turn and run away. Noike also froze as he tightened the grip on his walking stick and stared the fox in the eyes.

Neither of them moved.

The fox considered the little boy in front of him: maybe he could tell the boy had hit a rough patch, maybe he could tell the boy was just as scared as he was. The fox suddenly looked away from Noike, threw back its head, and continued on his path. The woodland animals would prove to be the least of his problems.

# 16

# WITHOUT A TRACE
*Florida, May 2006*

"You want to come with me on my walk?" my mother asked towards the end of my Florida visit in May. She had already changed into her walking clothes and was slipping on her sneakers. "I have an extra water bottle."

"Dad and I are going to work on the book this morning," I replied, with a tinge of guilt. My father and I had been consumed with the book over the past three months, not just during my visits but also on the phone, and via email and letters. I sensed that my mother felt cheated. I imagined her moaning to her friends: *My daughter came ALL the way from California and spent the ENTIRE time with her father.*

"Maybe we can go to the mall this afternoon," I suggested, knowing she wanted to buy some clothing and that my father did not have the patience for that kind of thing.

"All right," she said, seeming satisfied with the compromise. "It will only take me an hour or so to get ready after my walk."

That would give me two hours to interview my father. Without much time to spare, I immediately launched into the questions I had prepared about the events in Luboml and the neighboring villages. At first we discussed logistics—the distance between the towns, the size of the woods—but eventually we came back to his separation from Herschel.

"Are you sure Herschel was captured in Luboml?" I asked.

"There's no way for me to know for certain." My father frowned deeply, shaking his head. "Remember the body my cousins and I passed on the way out of Luboml? Many years after the war I met a woman in Israel who also saw that body."

The woman was Masha Ostik, one of Esther's maternal cousins. She had been hiding in Falik's attic when the Ukrainian police raided the first floor bedroom. Masha managed to stay hidden until nightfall, then fled down the same alley that my father and his cousins passed through on their way out of town. With an SS officer close on her heels, she slid under the bloody blanket and played dead. She later escaped into the woods and connected with a group of partisans.

"I wondered if the body under the blanket was Herschel," my father said hoarsely. "I should have asked Masha." She died about ten years ago.

Several months after my Florida visit the International Tracing Service in Germany announced that they planned to open their archives to the public. The archives were lauded as a treasure trove, an opportunity for the few remaining survivors to learn about the fate of their loved ones. With a renewed sense of optimism, my father submitted a search request for Herschel. A few weeks later he sent me the reply:

"A preliminary search of the ITS records and the Holocaust Museum's Namesearch database yielded no results." At the end of the email were listed other possible sources of information, sources that my father had already explored decades earlier.

No photos of Herschel remain, nor records of his birth or death; the same is true for my father's mother, sister, relatives, and neighbors who were killed by the *Einsatzgruppen* in Maciejow. The *Einsatzgruppen* records did not list the victim's names, only the number killed and their gender and age group. The precise location of the sites was also omitted from most records. In recent years a French priest, Father Patrick Desbois, started a campaign to locate and document all of the mass graves. The bodies are fully decomposed but the bullets remain, one per victim. Metal detectors are used to find the sites.

Without my father's memories and the memories of other survivors, it would be as if the Ginzburgs of Maciejow had never existed. This realization angered me but also reinforced my desire to write the book, to create our own record for Herschel, Blima, Pesel and all of the other lives lost in Maciejow.

## 17

# A BOY IN SHEEP'S CLOTHING
*Podswientne to Vladimir Volynski, Poland. October 1942*

About one week after Noike arrived in Podswientne, Mr. Shliva and Noike set out for Vladimir Volynski. They left at four o'clock in the morning, long before any other farmers would head out for the day. The road was dark except for a distant lantern every few miles. Noike sat in the front of the wagon until they were about to approach Werba, a small farming village known to have a strong police presence.

"Noika, why don't you sit down here until we pass through Werba," Mr. Shliva said, motioning to a spot on the floor where he had placed some straw. "If anyone stops the wagon, I'm going to tell them that you're mute." Even if Noike could convincingly lie to the police about his background, there was a chance they would detect traces of Yiddish in his accent.

Noike stepped down from the seat and crouched on the straw-covered floor. He sat there hugging his legs to his chest, resting his chin on his knees, praying that no one would stop the wagon. Although he had never met a mute before, he had heard one of the older school bullies calling another classmate a dumb mute. The boy was not mute, just shy and withdrawn. Noike planned to act like that shy boy, not saying a word and making little to no eye contact. He remained quiet as the wagon rocked back and forth along the bumpy country road.

Mr. Shliva sat upright and looked straight ahead as they approached the precinct, a small wooden building on the side of the road. These police officers were known to stop and search almost every wagon but they barely looked up as Mr. Shliva sailed through town.

"Noika, I think it's safe to come back up now," Mr. Shliva said when they reached the edge of town.

Noike pulled himself back onto the wagon seat and took in his surroundings, mentally noting landmarks as he had done in the woods: the house painted white, the fence with the broken post, the farm with the small dog. He tried to imprint the route in his mind in case he ever needed to return; he had learned his lesson after getting lost in the woods near Olesk.

About an hour later, they reached the outskirts of Vladimir Volynski.

Vladimir Volynski used to have over 25.000 inhabitants, nearly five times the population of Maciejow. The town was fifty percent Jewish before the war broke out; the remainder were Ukrainian and Polish. Jews settled there as early as the twelfth century and called it by its Yiddish name, "Ludmir." Homes in the outskirts of the town were typically one level, made of timber, and surrounded by small gardens. The center of the town was much more dense and had many two-storey brick buildings.

Mr. Shliva and Noike continued driving through the city, meandering down narrow side streets until they came to an abandoned lot.

"The entrance to the ghetto is over there," Mr. Shliva said, pointing to a large gate almost a block away. "If you need a ride back to Podswientne, I'll be back here next week, same time on Tuesday."

"Thank you for taking me here, *Pan* Shliva," Noike said, jumping off the wagon. Excited to be in Vladimir Volynski, he had hopes of finding surviving family members.

As he got closer to the gate, Noike saw that two giant metal doors were blocking the entrance. Next to the gate was a small, wooden booth with a young Ukrainian police officer on guard, wearing the standard issue black uniform. The officer reached for his rifle, stepped out of the booth, and approached Noike.

"Where do you think you're going?" the officer asked. He was skinny boy with a smooth face. Without the rifle he would have seemed harmless.

"My family is inside this ghetto," Noike said, as if it were true.

He looked Noike up and down. "All right, *malchik*, I'll let you go inside," he said, opening a small door next to the booth and ushering Noike through the gate.

Getting into the ghetto, Noike soon realized, would not be the problem.

Noike had assumed the ghetto would be open, like the one in Luboml, with the borders delineated by street names. But it soon became clear that Vladimir Volynski was different: the entire ghetto was surrounded by row upon row of barbed wire. The main street was dead quiet; nobody was walking around. Looking further down the street, Noike noticed a young man with a short beard who appeared to be Jewish.

"*Shalom alehem.*" Noike greeted the man in the traditional Yiddish manner. He had not spoken his native language in more than a week; the muscles in his mouth hesitated, as if they were forming each word for the first time.

"*Shalom alehem*, where did you come from?" the man asked, stunned to see such a young boy alive. All of the Jewish children had been killed in the earlier *aktions*.

"Maciejow, sir. My mother and sister were captured in the last *aktion*," he explained. "All of my other relatives were captured when I was in Luboml."

"It's a miracle that you survived, son," he said. "Very few Jews escaped from Luboml or Maciejow alive." Word of the massacres had spread to Vladimir Volynski via other Jewish survivors and villagers who had access to the ghetto.

"Have you met any Ginzburgs here?" Noike asked.

"No, I have not," the man furrowed his brow. "But you should ask around—I haven't met everyone."

"Is there some place I can sleep?" Noike asked.

Regrettably, the man told him, every room and bed in the ghetto was full. He explained how over 20,000 Jews from Vladimir Volynski and the neighboring villages had been forced into the ghetto last April. They were divided into two groups, exactly like Luboml: some got work permits; non-workers were sent off to be killed. About a month earlier, the Gestapo had ordered the head of the ghetto *Judenrat*, Jacob Kaplan, to provide a list of 7,000 Jews to be "deported." Mr. Kaplan refused to cooperate, committing suicide with his wife and son. The Gestapo punished the entire ghetto, massacring more than twice the number of Jews they had originally planned to kill. The population that remained consisted of young men and women between the ages of eighteen and thirty who were strong enough to work in the ghetto or nearby fields. They were moved into this smaller section of the original ghetto, cramming dozens into apartments that had once been single-family homes.

"You should talk to the Jewish police—they might be able to find you a place to sleep," the man suggested, pointing to the office down the road. The Jewish police was organized by the Gestapo and worked in collaboration with the *Judenrat*. If the Germans needed a certain number of people to work, they would ask the *Judenrat* to get the message out and the Jewish police to enforce it.

"God be with you," the man said as Noike walked away.

Noike went to the Jewish police office and poked his head inside. The officer on duty, a young man with ink black hair, was sitting at a small wooden table filling out some papers. He was wearing the official Jewish police armband, a white strip of cloth with a blue Star of David and the words *Judische-Ghetto Polizei*, Jewish Ghetto Police.

"Excuse me, sir," Noike said. "One of the men down the street said you could help me find a bed."

"We don't have any extra beds," the officer frowned, "but let's take a quick look—maybe someone is feeling generous today."

As they were walking towards the apartments, Noike asked about his family again: "Have you registered any Ginzburgs from Maciejow or Luboml?"

"No, I don't think we have anyone from Maciejow. There are a few people from Luboml, but they aren't Ginzburgs."

Noike nodded his head and pushed the sadness into a place deep inside of him. There was no reason to believe his family was in the ghetto, yet he looked for them still: a teenage girl with blonde hair could be Blima; a teenage boy with unruly dark hair could be Herschel; an elegant woman with chestnut hair could be his mother. With each turn through the ghetto streets, he searched for signs of his Ginzburgs.

He followed the officer into a two-storey house near the soup kitchen. Two to three people were already sharing single beds; newcomers had no choice but to sleep on the floor. Noike and the officer left the house and went across the street. They ascended a narrow staircase and entered a one-room apartment on the second floor. Five girls were sharing three beds: two beds were at one end of the room; the third bed was at the other end.

"Can this young man stay with you ladies?" the policeman asked. "He's traveled all the way from Maciejow."

The young women looked at each other and shook their heads. They appeared hardened from life in the ghetto, unwilling to share what little they now had. Everything precious had been taken away: their families, their homes, their personal possessions. What did they owe this stranger?

"All right then, you ladies have a nice evening," the officer said.

Noike and the policeman were about to leave when one of the young women asked them to wait. She was about the same age as his cousin Esther, with pale skin and doe-like eyes. Her hair was covered in a scarf and her face was devoid of makeup but one could still tell she was a beautiful girl.

"I'll give him my bed," she said, stepping forward. "My friends and I will share one of the other ones."

Noike thanked the girls and settled into the bed for the night. Ghetto residents were not allowed to leave their sleeping quarters after the evening curfew. Even if they had been allowed to leave, there was nothing to do in the ghetto but eat, work, and sleep. As Noike lay in bed he heard the girls talking amongst themselves at the other end of the room.

"What is the point of living now that my mother, father, and brother are all dead?" a girl named Rachel asked.

"You need to have hope, Rachel," her friend urged. "Some of the boys have been talking about an escape." At least two Jewish resistance groups were in the works in the Vladimir Volynski ghetto. Like the groups in Luboml, they stockpiled weapons and planned to escape to the nearby woods.

"What is the point of trying to escape?" Rachel snapped. "If the Germans don't catch you, the Ukrainians will. And we don't have much time left—now that the harvest is over, they don't have any use for us."

Noike flashed back to the night in Luboml, when he woke to gunshots at four in the morning. He tried to put it out of his mind and sleep but was constantly awakened by heavy footsteps. He imagined the SS and Ukrainian police barging into the room, ordering everyone out into the street. This fear would haunt him years after the war ended; he dreamt often that the SS had indeed captured him. "I'm not supposed to be captured," he would tell the SS officer in the dream. "This must be a mistake!" In the midst of the heated argument, he would suddenly awake in a pool of cold sweat.

Escape plans started running through his head.

Noike thought back to the time when the Russians occupied Maciejow. The soldiers used to carry around large shears to cut wire. If he could get his hands on a pair, he felt certain he could cut through a row of barbed wire close to the ground, dig a hole, and crawl through to the other side. He planned to search for a pair the next day, convinced that there was a way out of the ghetto.

The following morning, the girls told him that a meal would be served in the soup kitchen across the street. He walked over to the kitchen and stood in line for the so-called meal: a watery soup made with vegetable peels, the only food the workers would be given that day. The soup would keep them strong enough to work but not strong enough to run away, to fight off the police, to climb a fence.

The limited rations had created a black market in the Vladimir Volynski area: Jewish ghetto workers out in the fields would trade the last of their possessions for food; local farmers were known to offer a few potatoes or a sack of flour in exchange for a watch, a gold ring, a locket. One young man tried to smuggle a few potatoes into the ghetto, hiding them inside his jacket. He was caught at the gate and immediately shot to death.

After finishing his soup Noike followed the young men and women lining up for work. He stayed hidden on the sidewalk, watching as two Ukrainian police counted the group, starting from the back and working their way towards the gate. When they finished counting, the men opened the two large doors, keeping guard as the group filed through and waited outside. The police then closed the doors and marched the group to the fields to work for the day.

Noike considered joining the lineup the next day and escaping once they were out working in the fields, but he was afraid the police would notice that he was younger and they would stop him before he could even leave the ghetto. Instead he started poking around the ghetto, looking for anything that might help him escape, including the wire cutters.

After hours of searching the streets and public buildings, he could not find any tools to aid his escape. He later learned that the ghetto residents had been rushed from their homes in the middle of the night, unable to take any personal belongings with them. And even if they had been able to take some tools, the guards would have confiscated them by now. Noike thought he might have better luck in the larger ghetto, the part that had been evacuated a month ago.

Noike walked to the edge of the larger ghetto and peered through the barbed wire fence. Aside from a large wagon parked in front of a building in the distance, the road on the other side was deserted. All of the homes were being emptied out and searched for valuables: clothing, furniture, silverware, samovars, glassware. At a former Jewish school items were searched, sorted, repaired, and cleaned. Several hundred Jewish women and a handful of men were forced to work there. The local Commandant's lover, a young Polish woman named Anna, was said to have the first pick of women's shoes and clothing. The remainder of the top quality items were sent back to Germany; the least desirable items were sold or bartered to the local Ukrainian and Polish populations.

Noike considered how to cross the fence which was made from two rows of wire slung relatively low to the ground and loosely tied to poles on either side. He thought he would need wire cutters, but when he tested the wire with his foot, the fence easily gave way, providing enough room for him to step over. He walked into the first house on the street.

As soon as he entered the house, he could tell it had already been cleaned out, cleared of everything the Germans had deemed valuable. All that remained were dozens and dozens of black and white photographs: weddings, anniversaries, birthdays, holidays. They were spilled across the floor, stripped from their albums, evidence that living, breathing Jews had once lived within these walls.

Noike went into the next house and discovered a sheepskin coat lying on the floor. Picking it up, he saw that someone had sliced the back seam in search of valuables. He continued walking through the house, finding some socks, men's boots, and military grade tape for sealing pants and shoes. When he went to try on the boots, he realized that he had two right shoes; Noike decided to hold onto them anyway.

As he was about to leave, he noticed a family portrait hanging on the wall in the large room, presumably the living room at one time. In the center of the photograph a grandfather was sitting on a chair wearing a *yarmulka*, surrounded by his children and grandchildren. Noike thought back to the scene in Luboml, when he saw the grandfather walking his grandchildren to the graves, holding one child by each hand.

He was instantly reminded that a family—this family in the portrait in front of him—had lived in this home and had been killed just a month ago. A shiver rushed up his spine. As he stood there contemplating their fate he thought he heard sounds coming from the wagon down the road. He dashed out the house, back over the wire, into the smaller ghetto.

"That Jewish police officer was looking for you," one of the girls said when he returned to the apartment. "He said he would come back later."

Noike worried that someone might have seen him enter the other ghetto, or that someone had discovered that he was underage and reported him.

"Where did you get that coat?" the girl asked.

"I found it in the larger ghetto," Noike said weakly, feeling guilty that he had taken something from dead Jews. "I'm going to leave next week—I'll need it when I'm hiding in the woods."

"Is that right?" she snickered. "You'll just walk out of the ghetto?"

"Yes," he said, not fully understanding why she doubted his plan. He had not yet resigned himself to ghetto life; he was confident he could escape.

Later that evening the officer from the police station returned. "Ah, Noike, there you are. So, I did a favor for you before, right?" he asked Noike, putting his arm around his shoulder.

"Yes, sir, thank you for helping me out," Noike replied.

"Well, now I want you to do a favor for me. A young boy from Maciejow recently arrived here and needs a place to stay—."

"Yes, of course he can stay with me," Noike responded, before the man had a chance to finish.

"Very good, then, I'll bring him back here in just a moment," he said, heading out of the apartment to gather the other boy.

Noike wondered who the boy could be—he secretly hoped it was Herschel. He imagined a reunion like the one in Luboml, when his brother suddenly arrived, eager to tell Noike about his escape from Maciejow. They would be together again; they would never leave each other. Noike stared at the door and prayed that Herschel would appear.

When the officer returned he was with Laibel Chayet—the son of Maciejow's main tailor—not Herschel. Laibel had always been impeccably dressed but he now wore a coat with tears in both sleeves and trousers splattered with mud. Noike knew the Chayet family relatively well: Mr. Chayet used to make him a new suit almost every *Rosh Hashanah*.

"Laibel, when did you escape Maciejow?" Noike asked after the officer left. He was eager to learn what had happened since he had left more than two weeks before.

"I was hiding in the Taub home when it was captured by Ukrainian police." Kayla Taub, the woman of the house, was Noike's paternal great aunt, his *Baba* Perel's sister. Laibel hesitated as he continued his story.

"What is it—what's wrong?" Noike asked, wanting to hear the news but afraid of what Laibel would say.

"Your grandfather was hiding there too," Laibel said hesitantly.

Noike's grandfather had stayed in Maciejow after the first round of raids; he was too sick to make the trip to Luboml with his wife. According to Laibel, when the police broke into the house, he had a heart attack and died instantly.

Noike was saddened to hear that his grandfather, his *Zeidi*, had died, but somehow relieved to know that he was spared the pain and humiliation that followed. He was also comforted to know *how* his grandfather had died; there were so many others whose fate was still unknown to him.

Laibel and the others in the Taub house were chased through town and beaten with sticks and rifle butts if they did not run fast enough. When they arrived at the synagogue dozens of other Jews were already there, guarded by the Ukrainian police. They expected to be marched to the graves but it had grown too dark for the *Einsatzgruppen* to aim machine guns at their victims. They would spend the night inside the synagogue—an extra few hours to live.

At some point that evening, a man in a Gestapo uniform entered the synagogue carrying a firearm. Laibel and many others immediately recognized him as Mr. Naiman, a Jewish man from town, but they remained silent. Mr. Naiman demanded that the Ukrainian officers hand over a woman, a Mrs. Naiman, for questioning at headquarters. One of the officers asked him to wait until their superior returned. Mr. Naiman threw a fit, cursing the officer in German and drawing his gun. They finally let him take the woman.

When the Ukrainian policemen on duty were called out of the synagogue a couple of hours later, their prisoners were left unattended for a few minutes. Laibel and two other boys climbed out the back window and ran until they reached the outskirts of Maciejow. The boys managed to stay together for several days, until they came to the farming village of Ruda, where they were chased by a group of Ukrainian boys and forced to split up.

"I hid in a cemetery one night after we separated—it was haunted!" Laibel said. "In the dead of the night, I heard the spirit saying 'Isaac, Isaac, Isaac.'"

"That was me!" Noike said. "I was looking for my cousins near Luboml."

"Nah, I don't believe you—you're pulling my leg."

"Yes, it's true, I wouldn't lie!" Noike said. "We were resting near the cemetery wall when I fell asleep. I woke up and discovered that they were missing. Isaac was the name of one of the boys in the group."

"You're making it up!" Laibel still wasn't convinced.

"No, I'm not! You'll believe me when you listen to how I say it, 'Isaac, Isaac, Isaac,'" Noike whispered.

"I've got goose bumps!" Laibel said, half laughing

Noike, too, had goose bumps, thinking about Isaac and the others. He had been there the night they were captured but somehow it was still unreal to him. They were beside him one night, gone the next. He continued the cemetery story, then told Laibel how the group was captured in Olesk.

"Where do you sleep?" Laibel asked when they had finished sharing their stories.

"We're going to share this bed," Noike explained.

"Oh, I'm sorry—" Laibel started to say.

"No, no, I'm happy to share it. We are like family—you come from Maciejow."

Laibel slept on the side of the bed facing the wall; Noike slept on the outside. The boys coordinated their positions, careful not to tug the cover too far one way or the other, careful not to let Noike fall onto the floor in the middle of the night. Before the war, Noike may have whined about having to share the bed, complained about the inconvenience. Now he relished the nearness and warmth of someone from home. Laibel stayed with Noike for a couple of nights, until he was able to find a bed of his own in another house.

"Noike, a woman from Maciejow came to see you," one of the girls in the apartment said a few days later. "Her name was Mrs. Gold."

"When was she here?" Noike asked. He had been away from the apartment for a short time.

"A few minutes ago—she might still be waiting out back."

The Gold family had owned the big candy store on the main street in Maciejow. Noike used to stand at the window and look at all of the chocolates. They specialized in the popular Suchard chocolates imported from Switzerland. After what seemed like hours, the salesgirl often invited him inside, letting him pick "just one" for free.

Noike dashed down the stairs and headed towards the back of the house. At the end of the alley, he noticed a woman walking away.

"Mrs. Gold!" he waved as he called her name.

When she turned around, they immediately recognized each other. Mrs. Gold ran towards him, hugged him, and broke into tears. She was much older, paler, and thinner than he had remembered, wearing a babushka and a long, wool coat.

"I am the only one left of my family, Noikele," she told him, stroking his head. "Come sit with me," she motioned to a nearby bench.

He explained what had happened in Maciejow and Luboml and that he, too, was the only one left in his family.

"How did you get inside the ghetto?" she seemed confused. No one voluntarily entered the ghetto.

"The guard let me inside but I'm planning to leave next week. I'm going to sneak out in this coat," he said, holding up his sheepskin treasure. "Do you think you can help me fix it and make it smaller?"

"It's impossible to get out of the ghetto, my child. The only people who can leave are the worker groups, and they are heavily guarded on the way in and out of the ghetto. You also need a work permit, but you are too young to get one," she told him gently.

"I still want to try and get out—please help me," he begged.

"I'll see what I can do," she said, taking the coat and promising to return it before next Tuesday. As Noike watched her walk away, he thought about his mother and how she would take care of such things: a missing button on a coat, a hole in his shirt. Part of him wanted to go with Mrs. Gold, to be with someone who could look after him, but he was determined to leave the ghetto.

Mrs. Gold returned a couple of days later with the coat. She had managed to scrounge up a needle and thread to sew up the back, but she could not make any major alterations without proper sewing equipment.

"Be careful, Noikele," she said, before saying goodbye.

The next morning, a full week after he had entered the ghetto, Noike put on his escape disguise. He stuffed the boots with the old socks and slipped them on, adding a few inches to his height. Next, he wrapped the coat around his body, using an abandoned piece of rope as a belt. The thick sheepskin helped conceal his skinny boy frame. He beamed as he looked at his reflection in the window, convinced that he looked older.

Noike made his way down the steps, struggling with the two right shoes at first, then gaining his balance as he approached the men and women lining up near the gate. The police had already counted the group and were about to open the two big doors that led outside. Noike stepped into the middle of the line, between two young women, and waited for the instructions.

"March!" one of the Ukrainian officers shouted.

The group marched through the gate until everyone had passed through. When the policemen went to close the doors, Noike stepped out of the line and started to walk away from the ghetto. Looking over his shoulder, he saw the two police officers shut the doors, then one of them move towards the front of the line. He turned down a street lined with abandoned Jewish stores and dashed into the first one he saw.

Crouching down close to the floor, he waited for the police to find him, to beat him up, even kill him. He imagined a lonely death, face to face with one Ukrainian police officer in this abandoned store—one bullet to the head. No one would ever know what happened to him. But the marching soon resumed, growing quieter and quieter, until they could no longer be heard. Slowly, he stood up and looked out the window: the road was empty.

Noike had left the ghetto just in time. Within a few weeks another *aktion* took place in the middle of the night, killing almost all 2,500 ghetto residents. More than one hundred Vlasovtzes—a Russian unit that defected from the Red Army and collaborated with the Germans—stormed the ghetto, crying "Hoorah! Hoorah!" as they ran through the main gate and into the buildings. They kept about one hundred residents alive to collect, sort, and clean the remaining belongings.

Noike left the store and made his way to the lot where Mr. Shliva had dropped him off the previous week. Aside from a few unfamiliar wagons that came and went, there was little traffic in the lot. He sat behind a shed and waited. Several hours passed but still no Mr. Shliva. Worried that someone would notify the ghetto guards if he lingered much longer, Noike decided to walk back to Podswientne.

He was already in the outskirts of Vladimir Volynski when he heard a horse and wagon coming from behind him. He looked back and saw a older woman driving on her own, dressed in a black blouse and skirt—the costume of a widow. Waving his hand in the air, he asked her for a ride to Podswientne.

"I'm going to Kovel," she told him, "but I'll take you until the road forks."

"Thank you, *Pani*," Noike said, as he hoisted himself onto the wagon.

They had been traveling for several miles, when Noike gestured toward the reins. "You must be tired—maybe I can steer for a little while?"

"Do you know how to drive?" she asked, hesitant to let a young boy take over.

"Sure, I've done it lots of times," he replied, stretching the truth a bit. The man who drove the official wagon for Maciejow's *Gmina*, the city hall, used to let Noike hold the reins. The driver explained that his job was easy since the horses were trained to follow the road.

The widow handed Noike the reins before they reached the town of Werba. Steering would keep his mind off the police precinct on the side of the road; it would also help him blend in, for Jewish boys were not known to ride horse and wagons. He gripped the reins tightly, ready to set the horses in motion.

As they were about to enter Werba, a wagon full of police officers pulled out from the police station and turned in the direction of Vladimir Volynski. Before the wagon drew too close, Noike lifted the reins high in the air and whipped the horses.

"Slow down," the woman ordered him, leaning back as she grabbed onto the side of the wagon. "I'm not in a big hurry!"

"Sorry, *Pani*, the reins slipped from my hands," he hurriedly explained, relieved to have made it past the police.

They continued driving along the same road until they reached the fork to Kovel. Thanking her for the ride, he jumped off the wagon and started walking again. He stayed close to the edge of the road, listening for signs of the police, looking over his shoulder every few minutes.

About five miles past Werba, Noike came upon a farmhouse with an apple tree out front. The branches stretched out far beyond the fence, bursting with dozens and dozens of ripe fall apples. They were the same kind they had in the orchards at German headquarters in Maciejow: bright red globes with small patches of pale green. He reached up and began picking some of the apples, stuffing them into his shirt and coat pockets for the rest of his journey.

Back on the road, another horse and wagon passed him, but this time it was a farmer with an empty straw cart. These carts were longer than most, equipped with an equally long pole designed to hold the straw in place. An empty wagon meant the farmer must have just delivered his load. Again, Noike waved his hand high in the air and asked for a ride in Ukrainian.

"I'm headed home, but I can take you to the edge of the village," the farmer explained. He was a middle-aged man dressed in coveralls and had a gray wool cap pulled down over his eyes.

As they were driving along the road, Noike pulled out one of the apples and began to rub the dirt off with his shirt. When it was polished to shine, he dove into the apple, making loud crunching sound with each bite. The farmer looked over as Noike devoured the piece of fruit. Noike sensed that the farmer also wanted to indulge in the tasty treat. He had planned to conserve the apples for a couple of days but he didn't want to risk offending the farmer.

"Would you like an apple?" Noike offered, digging into his shirt.

The man took the apple and ate it, then another, another, and another.

Between bites of apple, the farmer told Noike that he had to get off before they reached Eika since there was a strong police presence in the village. "There's a wedding happening in the center of the village today," he went on to explain. "You might want to take the smaller road that runs parallel to the main one until you can pass the gathering."

"Thank you, *Pan*," Noike said, handing him another apple as he got off the wagon. The ride and advice was worth the extra apples.

A couple of hours had passed when Noike heard another horse and wagon coming from behind him. Worried that the local police were on night patrol, he moved to the side of the road and into the ditch next to the fields. Craning his neck above the ditch, he saw that the driver was alone and dressed like a local farmer. Noike jumped up and sprinted towards the wagon, calling out for a ride in Ukrainian.

"Where are you headed tonight?" the man asked as he pulled the wagon over.

"Podswientne, sir," he replied.

"You can ride in the back," the man said, barely looking at Noike.

Once they were on their way, the man asked: "Who do you know in Podswientne?"

"*Pan* Shliva." Noike was afraid to say "no one," thinking the man would be suspicious if he did not provide a name. If he realized Noike was a Jew on the run, he could turn him into the police, receiving five hundred German marks as his reward.

"Noika, you should be careful," the man said, turning around.

In the darkness, Noike did not realize the man was Mr. Shliva.

"Next time be more careful. You could get me in trouble," Mr. Shliva said sternly, shaking his finger at him.

They continued onward until they reached his farm. Mr. Shliva wished Noike good night and went inside his house for the evening. Noike walked over to the small barn door but it was locked; Mr. Shliva must not have expected him back that night. He went across to the other barn and found a spot near the geese, gently placing his sheepskin coat on the ground, careful not to disturb his new bedmates. In the morning he would return to the woods.

# 18

# GUARDIAN ANGEL
*New York. circa 1980*

"Mommy, I'm ready to come home," I told my mother over the phone.

Even though I was almost ten-years-old, I was still scared to walk less than one block in our safe suburban neighborhood of Tappan, New York. I had spent most of the afternoon and early evening at my best friend's house.

"Daddy will wait for you at the end of the driveway," she reassured me.

All of the houses in the neighborhood were built in the 1960's and fell into one of two architectural styles: Ranch or Colonial. The Ranch homes had bedrooms on the same floor as the living room and dining room; the Colonial homes had the bedrooms on a separate floor. The streets honored our town's revolutionary history: Washington Avenue, Eagle Lane, Constitution Drive. My family lived in a Ranch house on Liberty Road; we proudly displayed our American flag on every fourth of July.

When the screen door slammed shut, I dashed across the lawn to the sidewalk, my first milestone. The sidewalk from my friend's house to the next one was lined with a giant hedge several feet thick. I tried to be brave, but I ended up walking in the middle of street, far from the parked cars, and whatever I thought was hiding in the bushes.

The next house, where the Kramer family lived, had at least half a dozen cars parked in the driveway. Their eldest son, Scott, ran his auto repair business out of their home, working on the cars at odd hours, day and night. When he was home, I often stopped to say hello, but he wasn't there that night.

Ten more paces and then I reached the Mendes house, the yellow one with white shutters, the one just before mine. By then I could make out my father's shadow, as he stood there waiting for me, near the lanterns at the end of the driveway. We both smiled when there was enough light to make eye contact, then I started running towards him.

As I plunged into his arms, he lifted me up in the air. "*Shana madela*, how was your day?" he asked me then, "Did they feed you dessert?"

"No." I shook my head, smiling because I knew he had probably bought Carvel, my favorite ice cream, on his way home from work.

We went inside to see my mother, who was lounging in front of the television, ready for the eight o'clock movie. "*Mieskite*, don't eat too much before bed," she said as we made our way to the kitchen.

Shaking his head and smiling, my father took out the whipped cream, the chocolate syrup, the chocolate chips. Together we would sit in the kitchen watching TV, eating our ice cream sundaes.

At bedtime we headed to my room, where he told me one of his stories about the little boy. Night after night I listened eagerly, but always knowing something was wrong: why was a little boy, almost the same age as me, hiding in the woods alone, away from his family?

After my father kissed me good night and turned off the light, I wondered what I could do to save the little boy. I turned to my main source of information in those days: television. Tabitha, from the show *Bewitched*, and Jeannie, from *I Dream of Jeannie*, could make anything happen with their secret powers. And Holly, the little girl from *Land of the Lost*, traveled far back in time, fighting off dinosaurs and Sleestak monsters. If I wished hard enough, I thought I could have all of their special powers. Squeezing my eyes shut, I would travel back in time, like Holly, fighting Nazis instead of dinosaurs, mean boys instead of Sleestak monsters. Throughout the war, I would be the little boy's guardian angel, keeping an eye on him, rescuing him any time he was in a bind. Soaring down from the sky, I would help him escape from the neighborhood boys who chased him, the boy who caught him at the end of the alley, and anyone else that tried to mess with him.

"Who are you?" the little boy would ask the first time we met.

"I've come to save you—I'm your guardian angel," I would reply, once I had dropped him into a safe place.

As I was about to sail back into the sky, he would ask: "Have you seen my mother—maybe you can save her too?"

It was then that I would realize I had failed, that I needed to go back to the basement.

Turning on my invisible feather shield, I would time travel to that fateful morning in late September, 1942. As I descended into the basement, I would scan every corner of the room with my lightning speed x-ray vision. Within seconds, I would find the boy behind the wall and his mother under the bedding.

Rushing towards them, I would whisper: "Little boy, it's me, your special friend. Please hurry—climb onto my back before the police come!"

The little boy would peek out from behind the wooden plank: "Momma, it's our guardian angel." She would lift the bedding and stare in awe at my great, white wings, which were visible only to them. "Oh my God, Noikele," she would reach for her son's hand. As the two of them climbed onto my back, they too would become invisible, enveloped in my soft translucent feathers.

The three of us would take off, flying through the basement walls, way up into the sky above Maciejow, toward a safe place in a distant land. They would be together; they would be safe; they would be happy again. As I rolled over in my canopy bed, I closed my eyes and wished for it to happen.

## 19

# THE LITTLE BEGGAR
*Podswientne, Poland. October 1942*

When Noike returned from Vladimir Volynski he resumed his routine of walking in the woods near Podswientne in the daytime and slipping into Mr. Shliva's barn at night. Armed with his heavy boots and sheepskin coat, the cold days in the woods became more bearable. When hunger struck, he would emerge from the forest and beg for food in the colony.

Most families would give Noike milk and *boolke*, small rolls baked on Friday afternoons. He soon learned from Mr. Shliva that the entire colony were Seventh Day Adventists. They observed the Sabbath on Saturday, the same day as the Jews, spending much of Friday cleaning the house and preparing meals. From the edge of the woods Noike could see the smoke rising from the chimneys, the sign that the bread would be ready within a few hours. He looked forward to his rounds on those days. The freshly baked treats warmed his body and reminded him of home.

When he closed his eyes he could bring forth the smell of his mother's kitchen, the warmth in his house on Friday afternoons. The baking process would begin on Thursday evenings, when they prepared the dough and covered it with a damp cloth, leaving it to rise over night. The next morning his mother and grandmother would braid the dough, making large *challahs* and small *boolkes*. They would also bake sweet treats like sponge cake, *fluden*, a flat, square cake with apples and other fruit at the bottom, and *kichlach*, round cookies.

Noike observed that people in Podswientne would say, "Praise be Jesus Christ," when they entered someone's home, and those who lived there would respond, "Forever and ever, amen." When he went door-to-door begging, he tried to follow their custom by saying, "Praise be Jesus Christ" as he stood in the doorway. At first most responded with, "Forever and ever, amen," but some must have eventually learned that he wasn't Seventh Day Adventist, that he wasn't even Christian. Instead, they would nod or smile, not always returning the greeting.

While Noike was begging one day he came upon another boy, around the same age, who was also going house-to-house for food. He had a crooked smile and big, round cheeks which were pink from the cold. Slung over his shoulder was a worn *torbe*, a beggar's bag, filled with all of the food he had collected that day.

"*Czesc*," Noike casually greeted the boy in Polish.

"*Czesc*," the boy replied. "How did you do today?"

"Not bad—I got a *boolke* and some soup at that house," Noike pointed towards one nearby. Most people in the colony were willing to give him food but it was still dangerous to shelter Jews.

"You should go down the road, to that farm with the big vegetable garden. The woman of the house always gives me potatoes," the boy said, patting his *torbe*.

"I used to have a *torbe* like yours," Noike said, admiring the bag, "but it fell apart a few weeks ago."

"I have another one at home," the boy removed the bag from his shoulder and stuffed the potatoes into his pockets. "Take this one."

"*Dziekuje bardzo*," Noike glowed as he thanked his new friend. Now he had an authentic prop for his role; he would look like a real beggar boy.

A short time later he went to a farm that was set back from the road, isolated from the other ones in the colony. There was a large courtyard where a group of young men were insulating a barn for the winter. They were leaning poles against the sides of the barn, packing leaves between the poles, then tying the leaves down with branches and twine to keep them in place. Noike walked past the men, who were too occupied with the project to take much notice of him, and went up to the main house.

A young woman was standing in front of the kitchen sink, dressed in a black kerchief, a black blouse, and a dark skirt that brushed the floor. A large wooden cross on a skinny black string hung around her neck. As she scrubbed the dishes, the cross swayed back and forth across her chest. Sensing that someone was at the door, she turned to face Noike, then jumped back and gasped. Before he had a chance to say, "Praise be Jesus Christ," she dashed out of the kitchen, into another room in the back of the house.

Noike stood there, waiting for her to come back, wondering what he had done to scare the woman. Moments later, a young boy came from the yard into the kitchen, the same boy who had directed him to the Shliva house when he first arrived in Podswientne. "Maria, don't be scared—it's just that little Jew," he called to her as he eyed Noike. He must have told her about the time they had met on the road.

The woman emerged from the back room.

Embarrassed, she introduced herself and explained how they rarely had many visitors at the house. She asked Noike to sit down, then poured him a glass of milk and pulled a *boolke* out of the breadbasket.

"What's your name, young man?" she asked.

"Noika Ginzburg," he replied shyly, swinging his legs under the table.

"Nice to meet you, Noika," she said, extending her hand. "Where are you from?"

"Maciejow," he said, immediately wishing he had lied.

"Maciejow? Is your mother Pesia Ginzburg?" she asked. "Pesia" was Pesel's Polish name.

He nodded his head, worried the woman might report him.

His fears were allayed when she spoke fondly of his mother. Maria had purchased fabric from her store a few times over the years. She often went to Maciejow to visit her sister, Hantzie, who made a living delivering milk door-to-door. Maria had also lived in Maciejow at one time but moved when she converted from Judaism to Catholicism to marry a boy from another village, a tremendous scandal at the time. This husband left her early on in the war since it was too dangerous to be connected to a Jew, even one who had renounced her religion long ago. The Dzengelewski family took Maria in around that time, hiring her to help with household chores in exchange for room and board.

Sensing he could trust Maria, Noike explained what had happened to his mother and the rest of his family.

"If you can wait a little while longer, *Pani* Dzengelewska, the woman of the house, should be back from the market soon," she said. Dzengelewska is the feminine version of the name Dzengelewski. "If you have something to give them, they may let you stay here."

Even though Noike had the boots and sheepskin coat, he knew it would be almost impossible to stay outside once the winter storms began. "I have a couple of things I can give *Pani* Dzengelewska," he said, agreeing to wait.

A short time later, Mrs. Dzengelewska returned.

"*Dzien dobry*," Mrs. Dzengelewska greeted them as she set her bags on the kitchen table. She was a shrewd woman in her early fifties, with dark hair pulled into a tight bun and covered with a *babushka*. Her husband and sons managed the farm; she managed all aspects of the household.

She glanced at Noike, then fixed her on eyes on Maria.

"Excuse us for a moment," Maria said, gently leading Mrs. Dzengelewska into the back room.

From the kitchen, Noike could hear parts of their conversation. Maria explained how she had known his mother, how they were a good family, how they had all been killed in the recent *aktions*. The two women emerged from the back room a few minutes later.

Mrs. Dzengelewska spoke: "You can stay on our farm, but you understand it's very dangerous for us and we don't have much..." she trailed off.

"*Pani*, I can give you some things," Noike offered quickly, understanding what she had meant. "I'll come back again soon."

Later that day Noike went to the Shliva house to share his news.

"The Dzengelewski family offered me a place to hide but I need to give them something in return," he told Mr. Shliva. "My mother left some things in our house that I want to give them."

Noike wanted to give the Dzengelewskis his father's violin. His mother had kept it in the same closet as his old clothes and other memorabilia. Although Noike was too young to remember how the violin sounded, his mother would reminisce about the soft music that would fill the house and drift out into the street.

"I don't think it's a good idea to go back there," Mr. Shliva said. "There are still signs all over town listing the rewards for turning in Jews."

"But I need to get those things," Noike said with desperation.

Mr. Shliva tried to discourage him but Noike was determined to make the trip, convinced it was the only way the Dzengelewskis would let him stay during the harsh winter months.

"I'll take you to Maciejow," Mr. Shliva finally offered. "I have some business there later in the week." Mr. Shliva could get killed if someone saw them together and knew Noike was Jewish, and yet he felt compelled to continue to help.

A couple of days later, the two of them set out for Maciejow via horse and wagon. Again, Mr. Shliva told him: "If anyone stops us, I'll tell them you're mute."

It was a few miles down the road when they saw a young German soldier walking with a rifle slung over his shoulder. As they were about to pass him Mr. Shliva greeted the soldier in German; ignoring the soldier would have been considered an insult.

"*Guten morgen*," the soldier replied with a friendly wave. "Hey, do you think you can give me a lift to the edge of town?" the soldier asked. "I'm supposed to be on duty soon but I'm running late."

"Sure, of course, please come," Mr. Shliva said with enthusiasm, pulling the reins to stop the wagon. He whispered to Noike to scoot over.

The soldier hoisted himself onto the front seat. "*Guten morgen*, young man!" The soldier grinned at Noike.

Noike smiled back with caution. Behind the smile was immense fear and anger. The young man was an ordinary soldier—not part of the *Einsatzgruppen* killing squad—but he was still the enemy. Noike tried to look ahead and think of anything but the German sitting beside him. He prayed the soldier would not try to strike up a conversation with him.

"So, were you visiting a girl last night?" Mr. Shliva tried to joke with the soldier, desperate to draw his attention away from Noike.

"Yes, well, you know, I'm far away from home," the man blushed. "A friend of mine is covering for me until I get back."

Noike could not wait for the ride to end. He felt as if he was being pressed in a vise, with the soldier on his right, and not one inch between him and Mr. Shliva on the left. With each passing minute, the vise seemed to grow tighter.

"Ah, here we are," Mr. Shliva said, stopping just outside of German headquarters.

"*Danke*, sir," the man said, hopping off the wagon and walking towards the gate.

"Praise be Jesus Christ," Mr. Shliva said under his breath.

They went through the gate at the south end of town, passing the Ukrainian and Polish churches. Noike looked out of the corner of his eye as they turned onto his street, checking if anyone was standing near the house, but no one was there. Mr. Shliva steered the wagon into the empty lot next to the market and tied up the horse.

"I'll meet you back here in about one hour," Mr. Shliva said. "If you get here before me, wait on the other side of the street."

"OK, *Pan* Shliva. See you soon," Noike said.

Noike started to make his way back to his street, but instead of going directly to his house, he stopped at a Russian neighbor's home. They had been kind to his family early on in the occupation; he thought they would warn him of any trouble next door.

"Noika, I can't believe you are here!" the mother said when she saw him in the doorway. She was standing by the stove with her hair pinned back and a long, white apron over her dress. "Come, sit down," she said, waving him into the house. Her daughter, a girl of about twenty, emerged from another room. She too was shocked to see Noike.

As the three of them were talking, a young Ukrainian man came to the door and asked for the daughter. Noike immediately recognized him: he had lived in the house next to his grandfather's and was known to collaborate with the Germans. Noike tried to avert his eyes as he continued to talk with the mother.

"Well, I'll see you at theater practice," the young man said to the daughter before leaving the house. They were both involved in a play to be performed in the town theater later that month.

"He has a crush on my daughter," the mother said, once the young man was gone. Her daughter blushed and turned to leave the room.

"I need to meet someone," Noike said. "It was nice to see you again."

"Be careful, Noika," she urged, before bidding him farewell.

*Theater practice?* Thousands of their neighbors were killed less than one month ago yet they were working on a play. Noike could not understand how the rest of the residents of Maciejow could carry on like normal, as if their Jewish neighbors never existed. Taking a deep breath, he headed towards his house. As he was walking up the pathway, still lined with his mother's flowers, a teenage boy came out of the front door. He was the grandson of the woman who used to light their stove on *Shabbat*.

"You're still alive!" The boy turned white, as if he had seen a ghost. He expected Noike to be dead, like the rest of Maciejow's Jews.

"I just want to get a few things from my house," Noike said, sensing that the boy was wary of his visit. "I need to sell them so I can get some food."

"I have to get to school now," the grandson said, rushing off. "Why don't you talk to my grandmother—she's inside."

His grandmother must have heard the conversation–she was now standing in the doorway. A heavyset woman with graying hair, she was wearing a cotton housedress and a short robe. "What are you doing here?" she said bitterly, recognizing the boy who once lived in that house.

"I've come to find—" he started to explain.

"They took everything before I even got here," she interrupted, throwing her hands in the air. "I don't have any of your things!"

"But my father's violin," Noike said, trying to peek behind the old woman. "Can I check if it's still there?" He did not mention the silver and photographs buried in the back of the house. Most of the houses and gardens had already been picked apart in search of valuables.

"If you don't leave right now, I'm going to call the police," she said. A venomous look came into her eyes.

Noike immediately turned and ran away from his house. He panicked, unsure where it was safe to go and fearing the police would be out looking for him at any minute. He started heading back to the meeting place, walking quickly but not running, afraid that would attract too much attention.

"Noika?" someone said once he reached the lot.

He looked over and saw Elizabeta, the gardener's wife, with her daughter.

"Oh my God," she said, covering her mouth. "It's true—it's unbelievable that you're still alive. *Pan* Shliva told us you were here."

The gardener's wife had also assumed that all of the Jews had been killed and would never return. Her family had moved into a large Jewish home on the other side of the street.

As Noike started to explain what had happened at the old woman's house, he noticed Elizabeta glancing over his shoulder with a worried look. She looked down at him. "Noika, you must run—run, run now!" she said, pushing him away.

Ukrainian policemen with rifles were walking towards his former home, escorted by the teenage boy who now lived there. The boy was pointing to the house next door, then Noike's former home. The police were ready to hunt down Noike, to capture the one who got away.

*Where is the sixth one?*

Noike started sprinting through town, passing the gallows in the middle of the street, ready to lynch any remaining Jews and those who tried to hide them. He wondered if it was all coming to an end, if he would find himself up on the platform, a coarse rope tightened around his neck, the woman who stole their house watching along with her grandson.

He moved off the road and into a ditch that ran along its side, continuing to run until he approached German headquarters. He slowed down as he passed the main entrance.

Further down the road he saw a boy on a bicycle heading his way. When the bicycle got closer he realized that it was Volodia, a neighborhood friend who used to give him rides on his bicycle. Volodia was a few years older than Noike, with bright blonde hair and wide-set blue eyes.

"*Vitayu*, Noika! Can I give you a ride somewhere?" he offered in Ukrainian, circling his bike around Noike.

"*Duzhe dyakuyu*, but I'm meeting somebody," Noike thanked him. He tried to catch his breath and act as if everything were normal. No one could be trusted anymore.

"All right, maybe next time," Volodia said as he peddled away.

As Noike neared the edge of town, he heard a horse and wagon coming from behind him. Fearing it was the police, he quickened his pace, not looking back. The wagon hurried passed him at full speed and pulled into the Ukrainian cemetery down the road. The driver then turned around and started waving with both hands. Suddenly realizing it was Mr. Shliva, Noike raced towards the cemetery, kicking up dust and pebbles with each stride.

"Hurry up, hurry up—get on!" Mr. Shliva urged him in a heavy voice; sweat was pouring down his forehead. He started whipping the horse, getting it into motion before Noike had even reached the wagon. Noike sprinted ahead, threw his body onto the back of the wagon, laying low as he covered himself with bundles of straw.

Instead of taking the main road, Mr. Shliva steered the wagon down a side road that snaked through the woods.

"My eldest daughter lives near here—her husband is the local forester," Mr. Shliva explained, once they were deep in the woods. "You should stay with her tonight in case someone comes to my farm looking for you."

Mr. Shliva led Noike into the house and explained the situation to his daughter. "I'm not sure that this is a good idea," she said, glancing towards her baby girl resting on her hip, then back at Noike.

"Please, it will just be for tonight—he'll leave in the morning," Mr. Shliva reassured her. "You remember his mother, Pesia Ginzburg."

She agreed to let Noike stay but she would not let him in the house. Noike followed her to a small clearing behind the barn and discovered his home for the night: a giant haystack, bigger than the one he had slept in that night in Olesk. A wooden ladder was propped up against the side of the haystack, the only way someone could climb to the top.

"Go on," she said impatiently, ushering Noike up the ladder.

When he reached the top of the haystack, she removed the ladder.

"I'll come back with some food in a little while," she said, then disappeared into the house.

Noike spent the rest of the day lying on top of the haystack and reflecting on his experience in Maciejow: the look on the old woman's face; the threatening words; the police on his trail. He had witnessed worse leaving Maciejow the first time, but he was still shocked by what had happened that day. They had killed all of his people, moved into their homes, taken all of their belongings. Didn't they have enough?

He curled up in the hay and eventually drifted off to sleep.

The next morning, Noike discovered a visitor sitting beside him: a chicken had climbed to the top of the haystack. He observed the chicken clucking away, not a care in the world, her feathers softly vibrating with every breath. He reached over and lightly touched one of her feathers. She clucked loudly, stood up, and started edging her way down the side of the haystack. In her place, she left one egg.

Hungry, Noike stared at the egg and considered whether to eat it. He had not eaten anything since the previous afternoon; he had not eaten much besides *boolkes* and that one potato over the last several weeks. He tried to stave off his hunger, chewing on a piece of straw as he waited for Mr. Shliva's daughter to come with food.

One or two hours passed. Unable to wait much longer, Noike decided to eat a little bit of the egg. Poking a pin-sized hole with the straw in one end, he sucked out part of the yolk, filling his tiny stomach with a few drops of sustenance. He tilted the egg, with the hole facing down, and put it back in its original position.

Eventually Mr. Shliva's daughter came over to the haystack. She set the ladder against the side of the stack and climbed up with a *boolke* and milk. Noticing the egg, she picked it up, the remainder of the yolk dripping out into her hand. She didn't say anything to Noike. Maybe she thought another chicken had done it, maybe she realized the little boy had been hungry.

"I'll leave the ladder in place," she said as she climbed down.

After Noike finished eating, he made his way back to Podswientne, cutting through the woods until he reached the footpath used by the locals. This time, instead of going to the Shliva house, he went directly to the Dzengelewski home. Mrs. Dzengelewska was in the kitchen when he arrived.

"Praise be Jesus Christ," he said when he entered the house.

"Forever and ever, amen," she smiled. "You have returned."

"*Pani*, I still want to stay in your house—will these things be enough?" He pulled his mother's ring, watch, a pair of earrings, and a brooch from his pocket, gently placing them on the kitchen table.

"Those will do," Mrs. Dzengelewska said as she picked up the ring and brooch, turning each one over in her hand. "We'll take you down to the hiding place whenever you are ready."

Srulek, one of the boys in Malka's hiding place, had found the jewelry in a *knipl*, a tied-up kerchief, when he went back to Gitel's basement one night. He gave them to Noike when he learned they had belonged to his mother. Pesel must have left them on the floor before the Ukrainian police took her away.

Noike wished he could have held onto the jewelry—the last tangible connections to his mother—forever. But she would have wanted it this way; she would have wanted him to use these things to get through the winter. She would have been relieved to know that she had saved his life once again.

# 20

## REMEMBER YOUR FATHERS
*Podswientne, Poland. Winter 1942-43*

Noike stood near Mrs. Dzengelewska and peered down the dark hole. He had accepted her offer to hide on the farm but now, confronted with actually crawling inside and staying there for days—or weeks, or maybe months—on end made him feel uneasy. Hiding in the woods, though cold and dangerous, at least allowed him to stretch his limbs, to be out in the fresh air. But there seemed to be no other choice.

The hiding place could be reached through an opening under the *tzebrk*, a barrel that served as the kitchen sink. When the *tzebrk* was pulled away, one could see the narrow passageway sloping down from the kitchen into a room they had built underneath the pig and cow sties in the neighboring barn. The *tzebrk* was always filled with well water, which they replaced every few days. Food that settled to the bottom was mixed with gruel and served to the pigs.

The inside of the hiding place was about six-by-six feet and not more than three feet high. The Dzengelewskis had lined the entire space with straw, including the ceiling and the walls. One could hear the squeal of the pigs and an occasional moo from the cows above them. Occasionally, one could also hear the squeaks from mice dueling inside the straw walls in the middle of the night. A small hole in the ceiling allowed in air and a few rays of light.

Two women were already in the hiding place when Noike arrived: one was in her fifties and had a son, Shlomo, who had been a sharp shooter in the Polish army; the other was in her thirties and was a refugee, known as a *biezency* in Yiddish, who had fled from western Poland to Maciejow back in '39. She had rented a room in the Grosser's house, down the street from Noike's home. Her husband was killed in the first *aktion* in '41. She wore all black and spoke with a stutter.

The women had been in the hiding place for about two weeks. Their routine consisted of little beyond the basic necessities of life. On Monday mornings Maria would pass them a loaf of bread to share for the week. Noike, being the youngest and newest member of the hiding place, usually got the smallest piece of bread. They were allowed to use the outhouse at night, and made do with a bucket during the day.

Noike had been in the hiding place for less than one week when the older woman's son, the sharpshooter, came to visit his mother. He carried a rifle and showed Noike how to load it, engage it, and clean it. Noike was impressed to see a Jewish man armed with a gun—the first and only one he would see during the war. At the same time the power of it scared him, evoking memories of the gun held to his head, the guns held by the Ukrainian police, and the guns fired by *Einsatzgruppen*.

The sharpshooter and the two women left the Dzengelewski farm later that week and headed to a bunker deep inside the woods. They had grown weary from staying in the small underground tomb. Most of the bunkers were not much better than their current hiding place, but some were sophisticated structures built to endure the winter months, equipped with stoves and ventilation systems.

Alone with his thoughts, Noike reflected back to the time in the basement in Maciejow. What if he had attacked the policeman with the wooden plank? What if he had been able to distract them long enough for his mother to run? Deep down he knew any of his efforts would have been futile, but he still dreamed, envisioning what his world would look like if things had been different. For the first time he cried for the loss of his mother, the loss of his sister, the loss of his brother, the loss of his grandfather, the loss of his grandmothers, the loss of his cousins.

He could not shed enough tears.

A FEW WEEKS INTO THE WINTER, the Dzengelewskis started to invite Noike to the dinner table. Maybe they felt pity for the little boy; maybe they had heard his tears in the middle of the night. If anyone came to the house unannounced, they hoped he would blend in as one of the family: they already had six sons between the ages of eight and twenty.

The entire family sat at a long wooden table lined with benches. Most of the meals consisted of some combination of potatoes and meat. One of the older sons would slaughter one of the calves or pigs, and the women would then preserve the meat. They would place a layer of meat inside the bottom of a wooden barrel, then cover the layer with salt, continuing the process with the rest of the slaughter. Since most people in the countryside did not have refrigeration, this was a common way to keep meat edible for any length of time.

On Sundays, after the Dzengelewskis arrived home from the Polish Catholic church in Maciejow, they would make a special dish called *fusher*. One of the women would fry a few slices of bacon in a heavy metal pan, pouring the bacon and some of the excess fat into a vat of mashed potatoes. Flour would then be added to the remainder of the fat, creating crunchy dumplings which were also folded into the potato mixture. Somehow Noike's experience with the pork soup helped him overcome his aversion to the forbidden meat. *Fusher* would become his favorite dish.

The Dzengelewskis would serve *fusher* in a big wooden bowl, placing it in the center of the table along with a stack of wooden plates. Everyone had their own plates but there were never enough spoons to go around. The ones without spoons, usually the youngest at the table, would use their hands. Noike watched the other boys and followed their lead, digging into the big bowl with one of his hands.

Although the Dzengelewskis had their own farm, it was still difficult to feed a family of nine, plus one Jew. One night Noike and the older Dzengelewski boys took the horse and wagon to an area where Russian POWs had worked as slave laborers in the fields. The POWs had harvested potatoes the previous season and buried them underground for the winter. The Dzengelewskis knew the location and planned to steal some of these potatoes.

Tadek, the eldest Dzengelewski son, brought a bayonet and rifle. He kept on the lookout while Marek and Pawel, two of his younger brothers, uncovered one of the ditches filled with potatoes. The Germans rarely visited such remote areas at night, but the boys were still nervous about stealing. Peasants who stole from the German Army were known to be shot on sight.

"Noika, you stand near the wagon," Tadek said. "Marek and Pawel will pass you the potatoes." As Noike grabbed the potatoes and heaved them onto the wagon, he joined the boys as they sang a popular song in their village:

# NOIKE

*A thousand bombers, a thousand bombers,*
*Flying to Berlin, Berlin is burning,*
*Hamburg is collapsing,*
*Palaces are pulverizing,*
*Germans are running away,*
*What a miracle! What a miracle!*

The potatoes would last the family all winter.

After dinner one night, the Dzengelewski family gathered around the table, which was illuminated by a single oil lamp. Mrs. Dzengelewska was spinning wool with her spindle; the boys were singing folk songs with their father. Noike sat quietly, observing this peaceful scene and trying to understand why this family and many others could go on living their lives while his family was now dead.

It was a couple of months later, in late December, when a big snowstorm hit the region. Several inches of snow accumulated on the ground, covering almost half of the kitchen window. The Dzengelewskis had further relaxed the rules with Noike, allowing him to sleep in the boys' room most nights, on two wooden chairs pushed together. Mr. and Mrs. Dzengelewska slept in one corner in the kitchen.

In the middle of the night, Noike heard someone knocking on one of the windows. Thinking this person might be a Ukrainian police officer or a German soldier, he lay there frozen, wondering if he should try to escape. He could roll onto the floor, crawl towards the back of house, climb out the window, and run into the woods.

*I was always looking for a way out.*

The knocking continued, along with a muffled conversation. Noike thought the voices may have been speaking Yiddish but it could have been German. He remained motionless, afraid to run to the back of the house, afraid to approach the window and face the mysterious visitors.

Mr. Dzengelewski got up and opened the front door.

Two Jewish boys wearing newsboy caps, heavy boots, and wool coats stepped into the kitchen. Mr. Dzengelewski immediately recognized the boys and shook their hands. Noike also recognized them: they had lived down the street from him in Maciejow. They were in their twenties and involved in fruit merchandising—they rented out orchards out for the season based on past harvests. A few weeks before the last *aktion* in Maciejow, Noike had helped them pack crates of cherries. Their names were Yontzie Kalatzki and Lieber Indk.

The boys glanced at Noike, who was peeking out from the back room. At first they assumed he was one of the Dzengelewski sons but then realized it was little Noike from Maciejow. They nodded his way, indicating that they had recognized him, but kept silent. For all they knew, Noike could have been lying to the Dzengelewskis, posing as a poor Polish Catholic boy. They went over to the sink to help Mr. Dzengelewski move the barrel, then climbed down into the hiding place.

The following morning Noike joined the boys down in the hiding place. He listened to their stories and told them about his experiences since leaving Maciejow. They told Noike that the Dzengelewskis were also hiding a young woman and her infant daughter under another barn. Noike was familiar with the woman—her father was the *chazzan* at the Trysker synagogue in Maciejow. Without the Dzengelewskis knowing, she had allowed two teenaged girls from the village of Dolsk into the hiding place. Food had grown scarce since they arrived and the Dzengelewskis barely provided enough for one adult and a child.

Noike offered to beg for more food, as he did when he first arrived in Podswientne. Worried that he might cause trouble for the Dzengelewskis if he begged near the colony, he ventured further afield, towards a small Polish Catholic village about five miles away.

"*Dzien dobry*," he greeted one housewife as he stood in her doorway.

She was a young woman but she appeared older than her years, worn from her backbreaking work in the fields and running a household with several young children. The woman stared down at Noike's bag, then back at Noike.

"It's you," she said, spitting on the floor, "that little Jewish boy telling people that you're my son, that you come from our village."

Noike suddenly realized that he was in the beggar boy's home. When a few people asked where he was from, he had used the boy's last name and town to identify himself.

"If you ever do that again, I'm going to report you to the police," she said, shaking her fist at him. "Do you understand?"

"Yes, *Pani*, I'm very sorry. I promise I won't do it again," he said, backing out of the door and running away.

Noike returned to the Dzengelewski farm and handed the boys the bread and potatoes he had collected. They would bring it to the girls later that night. In the days that followed, Noike went out a couple more times, staying far away from the beggar boy's village.

When the three of them were down in the hiding place, Yontzie and Lieber would share stories about other Jews from Maciejow. One was about a notice that had circulated through the town declaring that all *aktions* against Jews were over. Several Jews came out of hiding only to be immediately caught and hung in the center of Maciejow. Another story was about a Ukrainian farmer who betrayed a family of Jews hiding near his farm. The entire family was then killed except for one of their sons. The son and a small group of Jewish survivors went to the farm the next night, killing the man and burning down his farm.

"You're lucky to have found Dzengelewskis, Noike," Yontzie said, shaking his head. "It's still very dangerous for Jews."

The more time the boys spent with Noike, the more they worried about his Jewish identity. His head was uncovered, he spoke Polish almost all the time, he did not say any of his prayers—he even ate pork. "You looked like a Polish farm boy," Yontzie said after a few nights. "We didn't recognize you at first."

The boys wanted to make sure that Noike remembered where he came from, where his father and grandfathers had come from.

"Noike, come over here. We want to show you how to put on the *t'fillin*," Yontzie said one morning. *T'fillin*, two small leather boxes containing Biblical verses, are worn by Jewish men during their morning prayers. Yontzie first wrapped one box, the *shel yad*, on his arm, then wrapped the other box, the *shel rosh*, around his forehead. "Now you try," he said, removing both of the boxes.

Watching Yontzie he was reminded of his grandfather, Yakob Ginzburg, a religious man who would wear the *t'fillin* and pray each day. As he picked up the *t'fillin* and started wrapping them around his arm, he imagined his grandfather singing the prayers, bowing as he prayed.

*Baruch Atah Adonai, elohainu, melech haolam, asher kidshanu b'mitzvotav v'tzivanu l'haniach t'fillin.*

Noike promised himself he would not forget.

About a week later, the boys told Noike they were heading to another hiding place in the forest. They planned to reconnect with a group of young men they had met on the way to Podswientne. Several bands of Jewish youths had managed to survive in the woods since the *aktions* from the previous summer and fall. They were fighting for their existence but also staging acts of sabotage and reprisal against those who had killed Jews.

"Can I go with you?" Noike asked when they were about to leave.

"It's safer for you here," Lieber said. "People are freezing to death in the woods."

Noike was not adequately prepared for the snow and sub-zero temperatures. The Dzengelewski boys had convinced him to give away his boots and sheepskin coat since he spent most of his time inside the house. Even if he had those items, he would not be immune to the diseases and other dangers that came with life in the woods.

"And remember, we thought you were a Polish farm boy when we first saw you," Yontzie added. "If anyone discovers you on the farm, they will think you are one of the Dzengelewski sons."

Although he had nearly fooled his own neighbors, Noike still felt vulnerable in the Dzengelewski home.

Later that winter, when Noike was talking with Maria in the back room, an old man entered the house and said: "Praise be Jesus Christ."

The youngest Dzengelewski son was supposed to be on the lookout when Noike was out during the day but he was nowhere in sight.

"Forever and ever, amen," Maria replied. She looked at Noike and pointed towards one of the beds.

Noike dashed under the bed in the far corner, scooting all the way to the wall.

The old man wandered into the back room and sat with Maria. Noike soon realized that it was the Polish widower who lived in a neighboring village. He started talking about the weather, crop yields, and the children he never saw. The man was harmless but they would not take any chances. Noike expected him to leave in a few minutes but the old man continued to talk, and talk, and talk.

"*Boom, boom, boom,*" the clock pounded after each hour.

More than three hours had passed before the old man finally stood up and left the Dzengelewski house. When he was halfway down the front path, Noike dashed out the back door and immediately relieved himself in the outhouse. The youngest son was reprimanded later that evening.

A couple of months later, signs of spring started to emerge. The leaves on the trees were green once again, the grass started to sprout, the flowers started to bloom. One morning Noike heard a commotion coming from one of the barns. Two of the older Dzengelewski boys were helping one of the cows maneuver her calf through the birth canal. Noike watched from the barn door as the boys gripped the calf's slippery front legs. Within moments, the rest of the calf slid out of its mother and fell onto the straw-covered floor. Mr. Dzengelewski slapped his sons on the back, praising them for their hard work.

In the meantime, the mother cow was nudging the calf with her nose, encouraging the little one to stand on its own. After a few tries, the calf straightened its wobbly legs and took its first tentative steps. Noike stared in amazement at the young creature. Only minutes out of its mother's womb yet it was ready to explore the world. That evening, Noike decided to share his news. He too was ready to venture out on his own: he planned to leave the Dzengelewski home and start looking for a job pasturing cows.

# 21

## HURRICANE WEATHER
### Florida. July 2006

"You can use the Jacuzzi while you're here," my mother offered when I arrived in Florida for my third visit that year.

"Umm, I don't think so, Mom."

"Maybe you want to see another show downtown? *Pippin* is playing."

"I don't know," I said, trying to change the subject.

We saw *Mamma Mia* the last time I was in Florida. As I sat there watching the actors belt out their ballads and shimmy across the stage, I felt like a fraud. How could I learn about so much death and tragedy, then turn around and sing along to Abba?

"Let's talk about the show later—now it's time to eat!" my father said. "We'll take you to Red Lobster; they have *very* good fish."

Red Lobster was deserted when we arrived. The "snow birds" were still visiting their children in the Northeast; most would not return until late October or November. As we settled into our booth we could see the low clouds hanging overhead, the lightning striking every few minutes. It was the middle of the rainy season.

"What are you two working on next?" my mother asked over dinner.

"We're going to go over some things from '42, then start on '43," I explained.

I wanted to learn more about my father's experiences in the Dzengelewski house that winter. Although I knew it must have been a traumatic experience, I was relieved that we had made it past all of the *aktions* in Maciejow and Luboml. Every time I asked him to review those stories for accuracy, I worried that he would fall into a deep depression, thinking about his mother, brother, sister, and other relatives.

Primo Levi was one of the reasons for my concern. I knew he had survived Auschwitz and was an accomplished writer of Holocaust literature; I didn't know that he had killed himself until my father told me. "I guess it can be harmful if you dwell on things too much," he said after telling me about Levi's suicide. "If we need to slow down, let me know," I started to remind him after that. He always reassured me that he was OK; I acted like I believed him.

The next day I launched into a series of innocuous questions that I had prepared regarding the Dzengelewski farm: How many barns did they own? How big was the house? He brought out some sketches that he had worked on before my visit: one showed all of the buildings on the farm, another illustrated the layout of the house.

"All six of their sons shared one bedroom?" I asked incredulously.

"They were basically poor farm people; they even made their own wool. Mrs. Dzengelewska would sit at the table nearly every night and work her spindle."

"A spindle?" I asked, not knowing what one looked like.

"It was simple, a narrow wooden rod tapered on both ends. You know the spinning wheel we had in New York—it reminded me of my time on the farm."

The spinning wheel was a fixture in my childhood home, never touched unless it was in the way. I had always assumed it was purchased by my mother, "for decoration"; I never guessed it was something my father had wanted for sentimental reasons. That evening when I was putting out the trash I spotted it in the garage, floating in the sea of other items he had refused to throw away for reasons unknown to me.

Towards the end of my visit we discussed his departure from the Dzengelewski farm the following spring. "What kinds of flowers were in the pastures?" I asked, continuing my most recent line of softball questions.

"You know, those ones we had in New York that would make a mess all over the lawn," he absently waved his hand.

"Dandelions?" I guessed, tapping away at my laptop.

"Right, dandelions and little daisies," he said. "The stork was back, the flowers were blooming, and everyone was dead."

I looked up from the keyboard.

"I thought back to my mother, and I felt so sorry that I—" He stopped abruptly, then covered his eyes. "I felt so sorry that I couldn't do anything to save her."

Memory has no clear boundaries. I had tried to steer my father away from topics that might upset him, but something as simple as wild flowers had led to his mother, my grandmother. You were just a child, I thought, not quite eleven years old. I willed myself to say something meaningful, but no words felt worthy enough to alleviate his pain. And then the moment passed. He was wiping his nose, putting his tissue back into his pocket, and rubbing his eyes, as if to rouse himself from a nap.

## 22

# THE LITTLE SHEPHERD
*Podswientne, Poland. Spring 1943*

The Dzengelewskis could not understand why Noike wanted to leave the safety of their farm. When it became clear that he was determined to go, they made him promise to keep their identity secret. If he was captured, he swore he would not mention the Dzengelewski name; he would say that he had escaped from Maciejow and had been hiding in the woods on his own.

Noike had walked less than one mile outside of the colony when he discovered a small farm set back from the road and bordered by woods on one side. There was a whitewashed house surrounded by vegetable gardens and two wooden barns. A Holstein cow and a dog were tied up near the larger barn. Noike went up to the house and peered through the open door. A young woman was sitting at the kitchen table holding a baby, gently rocking the child as she hummed a lullaby in Polish. She had pale blonde hair pulled into a low bun, and wore a long cotton dress with lace-up boots.

"*Dzien dobry, Pani*," Noike greeted the woman in Polish.

"*Dzien dobry.* How can I help you?" she asked, looking up from the baby.

"I want to be your *sluzacy*." *Sluzacy* is a servant, which implied that he would help with other chores besides pasturing cows. It was common for poor boys to shepherd animals in exchange for room and board; the broader role of *sluzacy* was less typical.

"Is that right?" she said, smiling at the barefoot little boy at her door.

Noike stood with his hands at his sides, his back straight. He wanted to make a good impression while looking for his first job; he did not want to have to return to the Dzengelewski farm. The Dzengelewski family had been kind but he was constantly reminded of the terrible weeks and months after the *aktions*. Each time he passed the *tzebrk*, the kitchen sink, he thought of the cramped, dark hole below and the Jews he would never see again. He wanted a fresh start, a place with no reminders of his dark past.

"Well, I could really use some help around here," she said, looking around the room and out into the yard.

"My husband isn't home right now. Can you wait until he comes back?" she asked, rocking the baby in her arms.

Noike nodded his head, still standing in the doorway.

"*Prosze, prosze.* Come in, come in," she said. "Sit down while we wait. I'll be back in just a moment."

She left the kitchen and carried the baby into the bedroom. From Noike's seat at the kitchen table, he could see her gently place the baby in a cradle that hung from a hook above the bed. The cradle, made from the local pine trees, swayed softly as the light spring breeze passed through the bedroom window.

"I'm making some potatoes," she said when she came back into the room. "You must be hungry, no?"

"Yes, thank you, *Pani.*"

She went over to the stove and lifted the lid off of the pot. "Ah, they are just about ready," she said, poking one with a wooden spoon.

"What's your name?" she asked, turning from the stove.

"Noika."

"Nice to meet you, Noika. My name is *Pani* Huber."

She brought over a plate of steaming potatoes, which she had drizzled with fresh poppy seed oil. Noike learned that the man of the house was an inventor and shrewd businessman. He had created a contraption, using a tree stump and pulleys, that could efficiently squeeze oil from seeds. Farmers from all over the region would hire him to press a variety of seed types: sesame, sunflower, poppy.

A short time later, Mr. Huber came walking up the path to the house, carrying a couple of burlap sacks over his shoulder. He was in his early thirties and had neatly trimmed brown hair and a clean-shaven face.

"Stay here for a moment," Mrs. Huber said, running out to meet him.

Noike watched the woman happily sharing the good fortune with her husband. The man stood there, nodding his head and smiling, seemingly agreeable with whatever his wife had told him.

As the two of them entered the house, the smile disappeared from his face.

The husband looked at Noike, then back at his wife. "*To ten zydek,*" he said, shaking his head. "It's that little Jew!"

Noike did not recognize the man at first, but soon realized that Mr. Huber was the same man he had encountered a few months earlier. Noike had been sitting in the sun near the edge of the woods trying to get warm when he spotted Mr. Huber and a woman from the colony stealing a tree stump nearby; they had feared that Noike was with the forester office. The woman had also said, "*To ten zydek.* It's that little Jew!"

Noike stood up to leave the house.

As he was about to head outside Mr. Huber asked him to wait, saying, "You know my father lives in a small village about twenty miles away." The farmer paused for a moment, then glanced at his wife. "He might be willing to take you to his village, then bring you back here the following week."

Noike understood his reasoning. If the Germans or Ukrainian police threatened to punish Mr. Huber for keeping a Jew on his farm, he could feign ignorance, insist that his father had found the little boy in another village, that he had no idea he was a Jew.

Noike agreed to go along with Mr. Huber's plan.

When he told the Dzengelewskis the news, they were quick to voice their reservations. "Huber sounds like a German name, Noika," Mrs. Dzengelewska said. They feared the family was *Volksdeutsche*, ethnic Germans who had settled in Poland centuries ago. *Volksdeutsche* were given preferential treatment by the Germans and were known to collaborate with the SS and Ukrainian police. Some *Volksdeutsche* had even volunteered to serve in the SS.

Noike sensed that the Hubers were decent people; he refused to go back on his word. Beside that he was eager to start taking care of himself, to make a life of his own. He had finally resigned himself to his fate. It was clear that no one would come to rescue him; no one would bring back his family.

Noike returned to the Huber farm a few days later. Mr. Huber's father was waiting out front with a horse and covered wagon. He took Noike to his home, which was nestled in a quiet village and far from the other houses and farms. Spring was finally in full swing: with permission from the elder Hubers, Noike climbed their cherry tree, squeezed through the branches, and searched for the ripest fruit.

Noike returned to Podswientne a week later.

"Do you have any questions about pasturing the animals?" Mr. Huber asked Noike that first night.

"Don't worry, *Pan* Huber," Noike said with confidence. "We had *lots* of cows in Maciejow." Over the years he had seen many young boys pasturing all sorts of animals but he had never done so himself. He was afraid Mr. Huber would change his mind if he realized that Noike had absolutely no experience.

"All right," Mr. Huber chuckled, knowing that few Jews came in contact with cows. "Well, make sure you bring the cow back for the afternoon milking."

Noike would begin work the following day.

The Hubers were still asleep when Noike left the house and gathered the animals. After passing through the Huber property and a neighboring field, he came upon a grassy pasture close to the woods. He released the cow and let her wander into a patch of tall grass. The sheep jostled each other as they made their way to the shorter grass inside the woods. Noike sat under a tree and watched the animals graze.

Later that morning another shepherd approached the pasture and sat with Noike.

"*Czesc*," the shepherd said, nodding at Noike. "My name is Pawel. Are those your sheep?"

"Oh, yes, I work for the Huber family," Noike said, proud of his new job. "My name is Noike."

Pawel was a few years older than Noike and had the aura of an experienced shepherd. He had collected a bunch of the long, white roots produced by young pine trees, and was weaving them to make a basket.

"Can you show me how to do that?" Noike asked, eager to learn the craft.

"Sure, it's easy," Pawel said, explaining step-by-step as he expertly weaved the roots together.

When Pawel was done with his lesson, Noike turned to check on wwwthe sheep.

"*Psia krew*! Bloody sheep!" he yelled.

"Don't worry," Pawel said. "You'll find them."

Noike went into the woods but the sheep were nowhere in sight. If they wandered too far off, he feared someone might steal them. If he returned to the Hubers without the sheep, he was certain they would throw him out of the house, maybe even kill him.

Worried that the sheep would stray even further if he waited any longer, he decided it was better to tell the Hubers right away.

"*Pan* Huber," he cried, as he burst into the house. "The sheep—they disappeared! I don't know where they are."

As he tried to catch his breath, he realized that Mrs. Shliva was at the house. She must have come to check on him, to make sure that the Hubers were treating him well. The Shlivas had also expressed concern over Noike working for the Hubers.

"*Dzien Dobry*, Noika," Mrs. Shliva smiled.

"*Dzien Dobry, Pani* Shliva," he replied shyly, embarrassed by the situation.

"Oh, they like to do that sometimes," Mr. Huber said with a chuckle, not a trace of anger in his voice. "Come, I'll help you find them." He led Noike to a small valley behind their farm where he had planted *kasha*—buckwheat groats—before the winter. They found all of the sheep gathered there, feasting on the new growth.

Along with the new kasha came dandelions and other wild flowers. One morning when Noike was out in the pastures watching the cow and sheep and observing the flowers, he heard a sharp clicking noise familiar to him. Again, he heard the noise: *click, click*. He looked over and discovered a tall white stork back from its winter migration, searching for food.

Noike was reminded of the storks near the lake in Maciejow where his family would swim every summer. He envisioned his mother sitting on the grass with her legs stretched out, waving at him as he dove under the water to let him know that she was watching. Thoughts like those would put him in a trance that took him back to how things had been, only to remind him how much had been destroyed. It was best not to think of any of it, not to allow the thoughts to run their own course. Immersed deep in the farm work, in the pastures, he was safe from the past.

A couple of weeks later Noike was sitting near the edge of the woods when a tall, emaciated man of about forty approached him. His hair looked as if it had been shaved down to his scalp and had just started growing back.

He was dressed in a Russian military coat, civilian pants, and heavy boots caked with mud and grass.

"*Dobry den,*" the man whispered hoarsely in Russian.

"*Dobry den,*" Noike returned the greeting, using the Russian he had learned when the Red Army occupied Maciejow back in '39.

Noike was scared at first but soon warmed up to the gentle man named Ivan. He was a former Russian Colonel who had escaped from a German POW camp near Vladimir Volynski. He was hiding in a dugout in the nearby woods.

"How big is your bunker?" Noike asked, eager to see one for the first time. He was also thinking about his future safety: if the Hubers ever betrayed him to the Germans or Ukrainians, perhaps he could hide in Ivan's dugout.

"It's nothing special, it can hardly even fit one person," Ivan said, sensing Noike's intent. "It sounds like you have a good situation on that farm—food, work, a warm bed. You don't want to be living in the woods."

Ivan had been subsisting on berries and roots he found in the woods as well as handouts from sympathetic shepherds.

"Please, have some of my lunch," Noike said, offering Ivan a piece of bread and fruit.

"*Spaseeba,*" Ivan bowed his head before accepting the food. They saw each other a few more times before Ivan disappeared.

As Noike grew more comfortable with pasturing, he started to take the animals further out, to pastures used by other shepherds in the region. While exploring one of these pastures, he came upon Mr. Shliva's teenage daughter, Zosia, and one of the Dzengelewski's younger sons. The two of them were friendly at first, including him in their conversations, letting him tag along when they went to other pastures.

One morning the three of them were pasturing when they came across a dark green snake camouflaged in a tall, grassy area. Startled, the other two shepherds jumped back, worried that the snake might bite them.

"I'll get him," Noike offered, beating the snake over the head with his staff. He whacked the snake once, twice, three times, until it finally stopped moving. He picked it up with his staff and brought it to them.

His two fellow shepherds were stunned.

"You shouldn't kill them, Noika," Zosia said. "The snakes serve a purpose in the pastures—they eat rats and other pests."

Noike was confused; he was only trying to protect them.

A few days later, they told him they were going to explore another pasture a few miles away. "It's a little far, Noika," Zosia said, "I don't think Mr. Huber would like it if you ventured that far off."

Noike was disappointed but at least he still had Rex, the dog.

Rex was a young collie with long, ginger-colored hair. The Hubers had kept him chained to his doghouse until Noike came along. Now that Noike was pasturing the animals, the Hubers were happy to have him out in the fields every day. Rex was happy too. When he spotted Noike coming towards the doghouse, he would jump as high as he could, until the chain pulled him back down. Knowing that a trip to the pastures was imminent, he would stop jumping and wait for Noike to unhook his chain. Once the chain was removed, Rex would take off and run in circles around the farmyard, eventually returning to Noike's side. They became a team, reining in the sheep together, keeping each other company.

Noike had always wanted a pet but his mother never allowed it. "*Feh*," she would say, "A nice Jewish boy shouldn't have a dog." Dogs were considered dirty animals. It was frowned upon to have them near the home, let alone inside the home. Dirty or not, Noike still longed for one of the cuddly creatures. Many years earlier, when he was picking up milk from a farmer near Maciejow, he noticed puppies running around the barn. "Can I hold one?" Noike had asked the farmer. "Hold one? You can have one!" the farmer beamed, delighted to give one away. Noike kept the dog hidden in his backyard until his mother discovered it and made him return it to the farmer.

After the morning graze, Rex would follow Noike as he led the sheep back to their pen and brought the cow over to Mrs. Huber to be milked. One afternoon when Noike brought the cow home Mrs. Huber was away from the farm. The cow looked like it was about to burst; milk had already started dripping out of her *doikis*, the udders. Noike had seen Mrs. Huber milk the cow dozens of times. Assuming the job would be simple—and he would impress Mrs. Huber with his initiative—he pulled the stool over to the cow and placed a bucket directly underneath her *doikis*. He went *kvetch, kvetch, kvetch* with the *doikis*, but nothing came out. The cow turned around and gazed at Noike, seeming to say: "You idiot, you don't know what you're doing. Why are you even trying?" Noike finally gave up. He cleaned the bucket and put the stool back in its place. Mrs. Huber returned a short time later and relieved the cow of her milk.

Noike always tried his best to do a good job–often going beyond what the Hubers had asked—but sometimes he made mistakes.

One day he returned the cow to her stall and neglected to firmly close the latch. Within a few minutes the cow unhinged the latch, walked out of the stall, and found her way to Mrs. Huber's vegetable garden.

"Stupid Jew!" he heard Mrs. Huber shout from the garden.

Noike looked through the window and saw Mrs. Huber tugging the cow away from the lettuce, tomatoes, and cucumbers. Terrified to hear the words "stupid Jew" and ashamed of his carelessness, he ran though the pastures and into the woods behind the Huber house.

He sat in the trees alone, wondering whether he should return to the farm, or leave Podswientne all together. No matter how hard he tried, he was still a Jew in their eyes—thought to be stupid and incompetent when it came to farm work.

It had already grown dark when Mr. Huber came into the woods looking for him. "Noika, it's getting late, come back to the house," he said gently.

Noike felt safe for now.

A few weeks later, Noike noticed a barren, hilly spot in the woods near the pastures. Edging closer, he discovered small piles of chicken bones littered about the area. He reasoned that a fox nest must be nearby since they were known to rob local farmers of their chickens. He started looking around the bones and quickly found the hole that led into the nest.

Foxes were valuable commodities in the region. Farmers who bred them could turn a handsome profit selling the pelts for hats and fur coats. Later that evening, Noike told Mr. Huber about his discovery.

"Let's go now—we'll bring *Pan* Swikla along," Mr. Huber said, not wanting to waste any time. Mr. Swikla was a neighbor who had experience catching and raising foxes. The men brought their dogs and a couple of sacks to collect the animals.

When they reached the nest, Mr. Swikla lit a bundle of straw and dropped it into one end of the foxhole, while Mr. Huber put a sack over the opposite end. All three of them stood near the sack, waiting for the straw to burn down and produce smoke. As the smoke started to fill the nest, four of the baby foxes ran to the other side, straight into the sack.

The fifth one, a young male, would not come out.

They waited a few minutes for him to give up but nothing happened. Mr. Swikla struck a match and dropped another bundle of fiery straw into the nest. Ten, maybe fifteen seconds passed but still nothing. They thought the last one might have suffocated when he suddenly scrambled into the sack. Mr. Huber kept three of the foxes, including the fifth male; his neighbor kept the other two. Mr. Huber planned to raise the two older ones until he could sell their full-grown pelts. He chained the youngest male to a little wooden house, as if it were a pet dog.

For weeks after the incident, Noike would hear the mother fox barking to her young. She must have been close to the farm—the barks were almost as loud as Rex's. The pups responded with high-pitched yelps, perhaps signaling that they were still alive and well. Noike had wanted to impress Mr. Huber but he was ridden with guilt afterwards; he never intended to take the babies away from their mother.

One of the male foxes eventually escaped from its cage and slipped into the barn with the chicken and geese. By the time the Hubers heard the ruckus from the barn, the fox had already snatched one of the geese and chewed its neck halfway apart. Mrs. Huber asked Noike to put the goose out of its misery.

Noike had never slaughtered an animal with his own hands but he had witnessed Jewish ritual slaughter. His mother would purchase their chickens at the weekly market and bring it to the *shochet* near the main square. There, the *shochet* would say a prayer over the animal, then kill it in what was considered to be the most humane way possible: slicing the throat.

Noike wanted to use the Jewish method but he was given an axe for the job. He looked at the poor goose whose beady eyes stared back at him, pleading: "What have I done to you?"

"Is something wrong, Noika?" Mrs. Huber had called from the house, wondering what was taking him so long.

"No, *Pani*. Huber, I'll be right there," he called back.

Turning the goose upside down, Noike noticed that her head dropped back. Not looking the goose in the eyes would make it easier for him, maybe easier for the half-dead goose. He raised the axe high in the air, said a prayer of his own devices, then *kaboom*, the axe fell, killing the goose.

Mrs. Huber cooked the goose for dinner that night.

It was around April when a stranger dressed in a sharp wool coat with metal buttons down the front came to the pastures.

"*Dobry den*," the stranger greeted Noike in Russian.

"*Dobry den*," Noike replied.

"Are you from around here?" the man asked.

"Yes sir, I work for a Polish farmer, Mr. Huber," he said, pointing towards the farm.

"*Volksdeutsche?*"

"No sir, they're a Polish Catholic family."

"Have you seen any Germans around here?"

"Not for several months," Noike said, growing increasingly interested in the man. He had overheard the Hubers talking about Russian spies parachuting into the area and establishing partisan units. These units were intended to lay the groundwork for the Russian forces advancing from the east. They would gather information about the German presence and transmit it back to Moscow's central command center; they also engaged in acts of sabotage, blowing up railroads and military bases. Noike wondered if this man was such a partisan.

They spoke a while longer before the man headed back into the woods, promising he would soon return.

Noike dreamed of joining the Russian partisans and avenging the death of his family. Partisans of all colors—Jewish, Polish, Russian, Ukrainian—fought fierce battles in the woods, swamps, and battlefields of Poland. But youngsters like Noike were rarely sent into hand-to-hand combat; the few who were chosen typically acted as couriers.

Noike also befriended an old Ukrainian shepherd named Stepan. The old man liked to make small wood carvings to pass the time: ducks, sheep, dogs. He pastured at least forty sheep and one feisty ram who threatened to charge Noike whenever he became too friendly. Noike often came up behind the ram, grabbed him by the horns, and jumped on his back. He would ride him through the pastures, the wind blowing through his hair, while Stepan kept an eye on his sheep and cow.

"I should make you a pair of moccasins," Stepan said one day, noticing that Noike's feet were often reddened and cracked by the cold, sometimes to the point of bleeding. His feet were often so cold when he pastured in the morning that he would step into the cow droppings to warm them, washing them off later in the pasture puddles. Mrs. Huber talked about making him a pair of woolen socks and clogs but neither ever materialized.

"Try mine on so I can figure out your size," Stepan said, taking his shoe off and handing it to Noike.

Noike took the moccasin from his hand and noticed that the inside bore Hebrew lettering. The shoes were lined with *dakkot*, sheepskin that had once been part of a Torah. Noike was shocked. The Torah was something sacred, yet this man had put it inside his shoes, desecrating its words with every step.

Noike was reminded of the scenes in Maciejow during the early part of the occupation, when the Germans were forcing Jews to take Torahs out of the synagogue and throw them into a fiery pyre. He thought of the old bearded man they had beaten until the torah fell from his hands.

"No, thank you," Noike said, handing the shoe back to his friend. "I don't need any shoes, especially now that summer is almost here."

A short time later Noike and the old man were sitting together when his sons came out to the pastures with rifles slung over their shoulders. Another shepherd once told Noike that the sons were members of the Banderites, a Ukrainian nationalist group founded by Stephen Bandera. The Banderites were originally part of the Ukrainian Insurgency Army, known as the UPA, the largest Ukrainian nationalist group.

"I'll be back in just a moment, Noika," the old man said.

The Banderites and the UPA collaborated with the Germans early on in the occupation, capturing and killing Jews who had escaped to the woods. Noike heard that local Banderites were responsible for bombing a dugout he had stumbled upon last winter. Noike had been poking around a grove with young pine trees when a Jewish man emerged from the bushes and urged him to leave: "Please go away and cover your tracks."

Noike glanced over at Stepan and his sons. He tried not to appear frightened as the young men gripped their rifles and pointed in his direction. The old man began arguing with his sons, throwing his arms up in the air. Noike couldn't hear what they were saying but he could tell the old man was furious, his face crimson with rage. The conversation lasted for a few more minutes, ending when the old man pounded his chest and shouted, "I'm your father!"

The sons turned away and left the pastures.

Noike was convinced that the two Banderites had come for him but Stepan refused to turn him over. Although Stepan never asked about his background, he may have suspected that Noike was Jewish. Stepan may not have liked "the Jews" but he clearly liked little Noike. His sons never returned to the pastures.

Later that spring word spread that the Banderites had reunited with the UPA and were planning to attack the Polish colonies like Podswientne. They were angered by Nazi Germany's decision to split Ukrainian lands as well as the ongoing exploitation of Ukrainian labor and resources. They had been willing to collaborate with their occupiers when a German victory seemed certain, but a series of major German defeats had signaled a turning point in the war.

Because they feared that the former Polish government would regain power and restore the old Polish-Soviet border, dashing any hopes for an independent Ukraine, the combined UPA-Banderites militia began to target ethnic Poles. Decimating the local Polish population was their preemptive attempt to claim the southeastern lands as their own.

The raids were to begin the next day.

# 23

# WHERE ARE YOUR GINZBURGS?

*Podswientne to Maciejow, Poland. Spring 1943*

"Noika, I have an important job for you," Mr. Huber said, the morning after they learned about the raids.

"Sure, *Pan* Huber, what is it?" Noike asked, ready to accept his new assignment.

"I need you to go up to the hill overlooking the road to Turichan," Mr. Huber pointed towards the hilly area. "I want you to keep on the lookout for any Ukrainian nationalists approaching the farm."

"Ukrainian nationalists" was a term that included active members of the Banderites, the UPA, and local peasants who supported their efforts. Mr. Huber and other Polish farmers had rounded up rifles and other munitions to defend themselves.

Eager to please his boss, Noike immediately set off for the hill, positioning himself so that he could see a couple of miles in either direction. His eyes darted back and forth across the valley, searching for any signs of the attackers.

It was a couple of hours later when Noike heard a shot coming from another road that ran behind the hill. Leaping up from his post, he dashed back to the farm to alert the Hubers of what seemed like an imminent attack.

"*Pan* Huber, *Pani* Huber," Noike panted, running into the yard. "I heard shots coming from the other side of the hill."

"Good job, Noika," Mr. Huber said, patting him on the back. "Help us load a few more things onto the wagon–we're going to Maciejow!"

Mrs. Huber had already packed most of their belongings; Mr. Huber had fed, watered, and harnessed the horses for their journey. Mrs. Huber's younger sister, Vanda, was also at the farm. She lived down the road with her parents and brother, who were devout Seventh Day Adventists. Her parents refused to leave their farm, believing their God would protect them from any danger. Many Jews had held the same religious optimism.

"Why are we going to Maciejow?" Noike asked, confused by the sudden departure. He had not heard about the trip until that moment.

"The German army has offered us protection on the Polish church grounds," Mr. Huber explained. "We'll stay there for a few days, then we'll take one of the trains headed to western Poland."

The German army was facilitating a mass evacuation of all Poles in the region. They were unable to control the local Banderites, who had become more powerful since they joined forces with the UPA. The combined Bandera-UPA movement also managed to recruit members from the Ukrainian police force and local peasantry. Many Ukrainian policemen had already fled to the woods with their weapons.

Noike was relieved that he could escape with the Hubers but terrified to return to Maciejow. He feared someone might recognize him, someone eager to collect the reward for capturing Jews. But he had no other alternative: he would surely be killed if the nationalists found him on the farm.

As they were about to set off, Noike asked about the farm animals: "*Pan* Huber, what will happen to the cow and the sheep?" He had cared for them for months and could not imagine abandoning them without food or water for an uncertain period of time.

"Someone will find them and take care of them," Mr. Huber said.

"Can't we at least take Rex?" Noike tried to contain his sadness.

"No, we can't take Rex either—we have to go now."

The four of them began walking to Maciejow alongside the overloaded wagon, which was too full to hold any passengers. Noike looked back at Rex, who was frantically jumping into air until the chain pulled him back down. Across from Rex sat his other friend, the fifth male fox who had refused to come out of his foxhole. Mr. Huber had tried to train him for weeks after his capture, showing him the same tricks he had taught Rex. But he would sit there, like a Buddhist monk in a meditative state, unfazed by temptation.

*Would they have left me too? If I had not come back from the hill, would they have left me on the farm with the rest of the animals?*

Noike had to assume that the identity of a Polish farm boy would no longer afford him any protection. Were he captured by the Ukrainian police, they would instantly know that he wasn't Ukrainian and take him either for a Pole or a "lousy" Jew whom they had missed the first time around. Either way, they would want to kill him.

On the edge of Maciejow the group's wagon rolled to a stop behind those of dozens of other families seeking protection. As the line inched forward, the entrance to Maciejow appeared as Noike remembered: the Ukrainian church stood to the right of the gate; the Polish one to the left. A Gestapo officer was standing in the middle of the road and holding a round sign that said, "*Halt*. Stop." Noike looked away from the officer towards the entrance to the Polish church and tried not to think of what others like him had done to his family and neighbors.

"What's your business here?" the Gestapo officer asked Mr. Huber.

"Sir, we are a family of five coming from the colony of Podswientne," Mr. Huber replied.

"Please turn left and sign in with the nuns," the officer said, ushering the wagon into the church property, then waving the next group forward.

Mr. Huber led the wagon towards the back of the church, where other refugees were parking and unloading their belongings. The church house, formerly the living quarters of a group of nuns, had been rearranged to accommodate the flood of refugees; bedding was laid out on nearly every inch of floor. Mrs. Huber went to ask the nuns about sleeping arrangements while Mr. Huber and Noike fed the horses.

"We have a room in the back of the church house," Mrs. Huber said upon her return. "It's over this way," she led them to the side entrance. Noike and the Hubers spent the remainder of the day resting in the room.

It was late afternoon when Vanda returned from a trip into town, carrying bundles of home-cooked food she had received from friends in Maciejow. She also brought along one of her friend's sons, Tomasz, who was about nine years old.

"*Dobry wieczór*," she greeted the three of them. "Little Tomasz begged to come with me—he wanted to meet everyone."

Noike recognized the boy right away. Tomasz had lived next to his grandfather's house. He often jumped over the fence and into his grandfather's garden, picking the ripest raspberries from the bushes. Noike had literally caught him red-handed several times: the boy would be squatting in the bushes with raspberry stains on his hands and face. He was certain the boy would recognize him.

Noike turned his head towards the window and looked into the churchyard. He could see the boy out of the corner of his eye: "Vanda, Vanda," the boy said, tugging her skirt with one hand and pointing at Noike with the other. "In our Maciejow there was a little Jew who looked like him." The boy was confused; he was told all the Jews had been killed. How could this one still be alive?

"What are you talking about? You're being very silly, little Tomasz," Vanda laughed away his accusation. "How can you compare one of our Poles to a *Jew*?"

The little boy looked down at the floor, his face reddening.

"Let's go Tomasz—I want to introduce you to some other families from Podswientne," Vanda said, leading him away.

Noike stayed in the room and avoided meeting anyone the rest of the day.

THE FOLLOWING MORNING THE HUBERS AND NOIKE WENT OUTSIDE to register with the church officials who were working on behalf of the Germans. The Germans wanted to track everyone who was leaving the region and make sure they had arranged enough trains for the evacuation. The church officials asked each person to provide their name, city and date of birth, and nationality.

"*Pan* Huber, I don't have a name," Noike said, pulling Mr. Huber aside. "What should I tell them?"

Mr. Huber paused for a moment, then said: "Stanislaw Kwiatkowski. Tell them Stanislaw Kwiatkowski."

Mr. Dzengelewski's name had also been Stanislaw. The name was commonly chosen to honor the Polish bishop put to death in the eleventh century and later canonized as the Patron Saint of Poland. Kwiatkowski, another relatively common name, literally means "One from the place of little flowers."

As they were about to approach the table, Noike froze. "*Pan* Huber, I'm afraid they might ask me questions," he explained. "Can you register for me?"

"All right, stay near the house while I register both of us," Mr. Huber replied.

Standing near the house Noike scanned the crowd, searching for anyone who might recognize him. Glancing up towards the hill overlooking the registration tables, he saw Tomasz's mother and sister looking down in his direction, marveling at the miracle their young one had witnessed: one of the Jewish children had survived.

Escape plans started running through his head once again. He could run behind German headquarters, through the fields and orchards, then back towards Luboml. Once he reached Luboml, he might be able to pass himself off as Polish Catholic orphan and board one of the refugee trains headed west.

*I was always looking for a way out.*

He glanced up towards the hill again; the two women had disappeared.

Later that day Mrs. Huber's brother arrived at the church with news about the massacres in Podswientne. Running through the woods, fields, and pastures, he managed to escape from the Ukranian nationalists who had killed his parents and many others hiding on their farm. "The Banderites bayoneted a baby girl to the barn door," he said, still in shock.

Noike was horrified when he heard the news, but not shocked: the German soldiers had introduced this sport using Jewish babies as their targets. He recalled what they had done to a young neighbor, Sara, who finally had a healthy baby after several years of failed pregnancies. The SS caught her during the first major *aktion* and tore the baby from her arms. "Please kill me first," she had pleaded, knowing death was certain for both of them, not wanting to see her child killed. Laughing, they shot the baby before Sara's eyes, then turned the gun on her.

The Ukrainian nationalists killed thousands of Poles that spring and into the summer. Noike listened to survivors discuss how Ukrainian peasants armed with sickles and pitchforks had forced Poles from their homes and savagely killed them. Beheaded, crucified, or dismembered bodies were displayed to encourage remaining Poles to flee.

History had already repeated itself.

Noike was stunned when he heard about Mr. and Mrs. Shliva. They had been passing through a Ukranian village a day or two before the raids when the Banderites captured them and split their heads open with an axe. Polish Czechs had been one of their first targets, given their nationality and reputation for helping Jews. Noike was not aware of it at the time but Mr. Shliva had also been assisting Jews who were hiding in the forests near Podswientne. Noike bowed his head and silently prayed for Mr. Shliva, a brave man who had saved his life more than once.

With many of his former protectors now dead or in danger, Noike was anxious to leave Maciejow, to leave eastern Poland altogether. If they decapitated the Shlivas, what might they do to him? He thought the Hubers would only stay in Maciejow for a couple of days; it now seemed unclear when they would leave.

The following morning, Noike went outside to take care of the horse. While filling the horse's feedbag he recognized one of the elder Dzengelewski boys standing nearby. There were no other Dzengelewskis at the church; the rest of his family must have already been en route to western Poland. The boys nodded at each other, nothing more–it was still dangerous to be associated with Jews, especially ones your family had hidden in their home for several months.

Noike was about to get fresh water for the horse when he noticed someone else staring at him: Olek Krajewski, the teenaged boy who had spotted him from a wagon in Maciejow and rallied his friends to chase Noike through town. He lived in the house next to the little boy, Tomasz, who had recognized Noike the previous day.

As Olek stared at Noike a Cheshire grin began to form on his face, as if he was saying: "I didn't get you last time, but I've got you now."

"What's your name?" he asked Noike, swaggering towards him.

"Stasiek. Stanislaw Kwiatkowski," Noike answered. Stasiek was a common nickname for Stanislaw.

Smirking, Olek asked again: "But what's your real name?"

"Ask him if you don't believe me," Noike said, pointing towards the Dzengelewski's son.

Olek looked over at the Dzengelewski's son, who shrugged his shoulders and walked away. The smirk quickly returned to Olek's face. He was now even more confident about his accusation, more determined to stick around and harass Noike.

Noike turned from Olek and headed back towards the church house.

Olek trailed him as he walked away, then asked: "Where are your Ginzburgs?"

"Ginzburg? What do you mean?" Noike responded with an indignant tone, standing face-to-face with his arch-enemy.

"*Ginzborgy*," he said, pronouncing each syllable with a strong Polish accent. "You know what I mean."

"No, I don't know what you're talking about," Noike replied, continuing to walk away, into the house.

Olek did not follow him inside.

Noike went back to the Huber's room and sat near the window, searching for Olek in the yard, planning an escape route if the boy were to return and terrorize him once again. At that moment, he spotted him near the entrance to the church property with another boy.

They were heading for the church house.

Noike moved away from the window and slipped into the large room across the hall, where a group of nuns were registering the latest arrival of refugees. Several Polish farmwomen surrounded one of the tables; their long, full skirts flared out, almost touching the floor. Noike made believe he had dropped something near the table, then got on his hands and knees to retrieve it. Once on the floor, he crawled between two of the women, camouflaged in their sea of skirts, until he was safely hidden under the table.

"There's no one here," he heard the other boy say to Olek as they moved through the Huber's room and entered the registration room.

"I swear—he was here just a few minutes ago," Olek said. "He must have run away."

The boys eventually gave up and left.

Noike tried to appear calm as he climbed out from under the table; the women were too immersed in the registrations to notice that he had slipped back between their skirts. He feared the boys would soon return with others, ready to hunt him down and get fifty marks and some sugar for their work. He went back to the Huber's room and waited for them to return from town. They had been running errands in preparation for the upcoming journey to western Poland.

"*Czesc*, Noika," Mr. Huber said upon his return.

"*Czesc, Pan* Huber," Noike replied.

"Is something wrong?" Mr. Huber asked, sensing Noike was upset.

"I don't feel comfortable here, *Pan* Huber. One of the boys from my old neighborhood recognized me. He left but I'm afraid he'll come back—I'm going to leave today."

"Wait a moment. Let me talk this over with *Pani* Huber."

Mr. Huber went outside to find his wife.

The two of them returned a few minutes later, carrying cloth bundles filled with food and jugs of water.

"We will leave together, Noika," Mr. Huber said. "There's a group taking a train that leaves in about two hours. If we start walking over there now, we should be able to board it."

"*Prosze*, Noika," Mrs. Huber said, handing him one of the bundles. "You'll need this for the train ride—it may take several hours to get to Chelm."

Chelm, a town about fifty miles southwest of Maciejow, was to be their new home. The town was located in an ethnic Polish region where the Ukrainian nationalists had marginal influence. More importantly, Chelm could accommodate a large influx of new residents: 18,000 Jews were killed the previous year, leaving an abundance of empty Jewish homes.

The Hubers, along with several other Polish families, began walking to the Maciejow train station en masse. Their arms were piled with whatever belongings they could carry; everything else was sold, abandoned, or given to friends who had made alternate travel arrangements. Noike lowered his gaze as they passed by his street; he tried not to think about his former life, his family, or his neighbors.

When they arrived at the train station it was bustling with Polish farmers carrying their most precious possessions, all patiently waiting to board the train to the west. Neighbors were hugging each other goodbye, uncertain when they would meet again.

"Noika?" he heard a familiar woman call his name.

Noike turned and discovered the gardener's wife, Elizabeta, standing with her daughter on the platform. Elizabeta had been good to him many times throughout the war: she had given him fruit when he was hiding in Malka's house; she had saved him from the Ukrainian police the last time he was in Maciejow.

"Noika, I'm so happy to see you," she said with a warm smile.

"It's nice to see you too," he said looking up at her. He restrained the impulse to be more demonstrative, fearing anything more than a casual greeting would attract too much attention and put them both in danger.

"I should go wait for the train over there," he said, motioning towards the rear, where the Hubers and others were standing on the platform.

"*Do widzenia*, little Noika, take care of yourself," she said.

He walked to the end of the platform and stood near the Hubers. When the train approached the station, he told the Hubers he would sit in a different car, in case one of the officers on the train stopped to question him. He promised not to mention the Huber name.

"All aboard!" one of the German officers shouted as the train pulled into the station. Tickets were not needed for this journey—the Germans still controlled the railroads and had guaranteed all Poles in the region a one-way ticket west.

Noike boarded the train carrying nothing but his bundle of food and water. He poked his head inside several compartments but all of the seats were already taken. Walking into the least crowded compartment, he moved towards the back and stood near the open window.

As the train started moving he was reminded of his last train trip, the one he took with his brother to Luboml before the war. The two of them had stared at the engine in awe as the big locomotive fired up, then fixed their eyes out the window as they passed through the vast countryside.

*Where is Herschel? Where is everyone? Surely others have survived.*

He felt a strange sadness as the train steamed ahead, moving further and further away from the place he had once called home. Maciejow had ceased to be his home the day he ran to Luboml, but in his heart he continued to long for the old Maciejow, where he had celebrated *Shabbat* with his family at home, played soccer with his brother after school, and wandered freely through the weekly market.

Perching his chin on the edge of the train window, Noike let the spring breeze blow across his face and hair. He closed his eyes and breathed in the sweet smell of the pine trees and wild flowers that lined the railroad tracks, imagining the old Maciejow.

"Luboml," the conductor announced less than an hour later. "We will be making a brief stop in Luboml."

Dozens and dozens of Polish refugees boarded the train, squeezing into the already packed compartments. Noike scanned the faces on the platform, hoping he might see someone he knew, someone who had also managed to survive: his brother, cousins, aunts, maybe even his mother and sister. But one after the other, a sea of strangers boarded the train—no familiar faces. The train continued onward, crossing the Bug River into western Poland, then finally stopped in the town of Chelm.

## 24

## TRESPASSING INTO HIS MEMORY
*On the phone, June 2006*

"Did you get my package?" my father asked me over the phone. "I sent you some more information about Podswientne."

"Yes, but I haven't gone through it yet. I'm heading to Chelm right now," I explained.

"Oh, you're not at home. You want to call me later?" he asked.

"No, I said *Chelm*, I'm immersed in your trip to Chelm," I said. "I can't think about Podswientne; I'll get back to that part next week."

The process of writing the book—of constantly looking backwards—was often painful. The more I understood the little boy and his world, the more I felt compelled to write him out of every chapter. I found myself surging ahead, writing furiously to make time move forward, to get him to the present, to get him to safety.

"Oh, I see what you mean," my father laughed. "Remember when we started the book and you said: 'You have to tell me what you were thinking, I can't get into your head.' Well, I think you're in there now, deep in there." My father laughed again. Then, in a more serious tone: "I can feel you in there."

Sometimes I worried that I had trespassed too far into his memory: Should I really be in there? How much should I know? How much do I want to know? As his biographer I realized that I should want to know everything, but many times I wanted to say: "Enough—don't tell me anymore!" Gang rapes, babies bayoneted to walls, people buried half dead. No wonder he waited this long to tell me everything.

But there was no turning back now. The more I knew, the more responsibility I felt to tell his stories—to tell all of their stories.

As the weeks went by and we delved deeper into the past, his experiences were gradually etched into my mind; I was assimilating them as my own memories. The places he visited, the people he had met along the way—I knew them all.

"You know Mr. Huber…?" he had started to say one day.

"Yes, of course I know Mr. Huber," I said, as if I, too, had lived on the farm.

Sometimes we didn't have to exchange words to confirm that we understood each other. Instead we would exchange knowing glances, our eyes brimming with what could not be said: "You know how terrible that must have been; you know that kind of terror can not be put into words." When he looked at me that way, it was the little boy behind those eyes, not my father.

"Eventually you will know my stories better than me," my dad said towards the end of one of our phone calls, a compliment that inspired and unsettled me. I wanted to know his stories *almost* as well he did; knowing them better than him reminded me of his mortality.

We grew much closer as the book progressed and he shared the most painful experiences of his life. It amazed me that someone who lost everything could turn into a model father who would help his children with homework, teach them how to swim, and make ice cream sundaes. Although I had always loved and respected my father, I never really understood him. Now that I did, I feared losing him even more.

# 25

## OF BLOOD AND BONES
*Chelm, Poland. Summer 1943*

Leaving the Chelm train station Noike noticed a row of abandoned Jewish businesses—a kosher butcher, a Jewish bakery, a *sheitel* shop—their windows broken and doors smashed. Chelm had been a Jewish cultural center for centuries, known throughout all of Poland for its Yiddish newspapers, synagogues, and prestigious yeshivas. Noike had never visited the town but his father had cousins who had lived there; he wondered if any had survived.

Noike followed the Hubers to a large house in the center of town. As he passed through the doorway, he saw traces of a *mezuzah*: the small, rectangular outline; fresh holes from the tiny screws. The former Jewish home now served as both a meeting place for Polish families who were separated during the raids and a placement center for new arrivals. Polish refugees were lined up in front of long wooden tables inside the house, where they waited to learn about housing and work opportunities; others crowded around message boards, searching for information about friends and relatives.

While Noike was waiting with Mrs. Huber he noticed Mr. Huber talking with an older man sitting on the edge of one of the tables. They were engaged in a lively conversation, talking as if they had known each other for a long time. As people walked into and out of the house, they smiled and warmly greeted the older man. He was the best-dressed person in the room, wearing a fine wool coat and leather boots with brand new laces.

"Stasiek," Mr. Huber called Noike by his new name for the first time. "Come over here. I want you to meet someone."

"*Dzien dobry*," Noike said as he approached the men.

"Stasiek, this is *Pan* Pyra, the mayor of Maidan, a small village outside of Chelm. He needs an extra hand on his farm—someone to pasture the cows and help with other chores. I told him how you helped me in Podswientne after you fled from your village. He knows what those *vicious* Ukrainian nationalists did to your parents, who were such devout Catholics, such good people," he said, stroking Noike's head.

"*Dzien dobry*, young man," Mr. Pyra said. "Tell me your full name."

"Stanislav Kwiatkowski," Noike replied, carefully pronouncing his new name, trying to make his accent sound distinctly Polish.

"Stanislav Kwiatkowski," Mr. Pyra nodded his head. "That is a true Polish name, a Polish name of blood and bones."

Noike stood there and smiled. Learning that his new name was the consummate Polish name gave him confidence and helped convince him that he could play the part of an orphaned Polish Catholic boy.

"You poor child," Mr. Pyra said, shaking his head. He got up from the table and kissed Noike on the head. "Shall we go to my farm, Stasiek?"

The Hubers were not granted farmland in Chelm, so they no longer needed Noike's help in the pastures. The Pyras agreed to provide Noike with room and board in exchange for his work in the pastures and on the farm. The arrangements had already been made.

"*Do widzenia, Pan* Huber," Noike said goodbye, trying not to show his regret.

"*Do widzenia*, Stasiek," Mr. Huber shook Noike's hand. "We'll come visit you on the Pyra farm."

Noike was disappointed that he could not stay with the Huber family—the only people who knew about his past and the only people he knew he could trust. But he had grown accustomed to moving around, severing old connections. Moving gave him a certain distance from his old life, a distance that would serve to protect him.

"We live on Piwna Road," Mr. Pyra said as they drove to the farm, about ten minutes outside of Chelm. "It's easy to remember since we're next to the Piviarnia beer factory."

Noike later learned that the factory was owned by Jews until the Gestapo arrested and murdered the family in 1942. The Gestapo also confiscated a Jewish-owned whiskey factory, Gurzelnia, around that time. Further down the road, past the beer factory, were the German army barracks, the same barracks used by the Polish army before the war.

When they reached Piwna #20, Mr. Pyra turned left and parked the wagon.

The Pyra farm had three long wooden barns: one for storing grain; another for working inside during the winter; and a third for the cows, horses, pigs, and countless chickens, geese, and ducks. The main house was made from brick and had four rooms, twice the size of the Huber home. About a half dozen fruit trees—apple, pear, cherry—surrounded the house.

Noike met the rest of the Pyra family at dinner that evening.

"Stasiek, this is my wife, *Pani* Pyra," Mr. Pyra said, introducing a petite woman with heavy eyelids and pitch-black hair that she wore in a bun.

"*Dzien dobry*," Mrs. Pyra said as she set platters of homemade sausage and cheese on the table. She was reserved that first night, hardly saying a word while she served and ate the meal.

"Hello, Stasiek, I'm Marisia." Their only daughter stood up to greet Noike. She was twenty years old, with a tiny nose and pale blonde hair.

"And these are my sons—Zbysiek and Kazik," Mr. Pyra said, gesturing towards the boys. Zbysiek, a muscular boy in his early twenties, worked out in the fields most of the day, farming wheat and barley. Kazik had recently turned eighteen years old, and worked at the railroad station as an electrician.

After dinner Mr. Pyra told his children to get their musical instruments—Zbysiek played guitar, Kazik the violin, and Marisia the mandolin.

"Do you like music, Stasiek?" Mr. Pyra asked.

"Of course," Noike replied, delighted by the warm welcome.

"Wonderful—we'll play one of my favorites, a song I learned when I served in the Tzarist army in the First World War."

Mr. Pyra nodded towards his children as a cue, then sang in a deep soulful voice:

> *The evening is approaching, the grass is swaying*
> *My dear one is not coming*
> *I will go to him myself…*

That night, Noike slept in his new bed: three wooden chairs pushed together next to the kitchen stove. Zbysiek slept in the other corner of the kitchen on a narrow bed with a straw mattress. Before they went to sleep,

Noike watched Zbysiek kneel beside the bed, place his palms together, and say his evening prayers. Noike also got on his knees, but instead of praying he argued with his God. He demanded to know why his family and neighbors had been killed, why he was left to suffer all alone.

There were still no answers.

THE NEXT MORNING NOIKE TOOK THE COWS OUT FROM THEIR STALL, leading them to the pastures on the other side of the railroad tracks. Nearing the tracks, Noike slowed as he came upon the remnants of an accident: several train cars were smashed to pieces and lying across the tracks; insulation from the cars was littered everywhere. A couple of men were standing around the cars, discussing the best way to remove them.

"Son, you need to go around," one of the men said, noticing that Noike was staring at the site. "We'll have the cars removed by tomorrow morning."

Noike learned that local Polish partisans had blown up the train. The dominant Polish partisan movement was known as the *Armia Krajowa,* or AK. The AK's primary goal was to sabotage the Nazis and reinstate the former Polish government. With the help of secret couriers, they maintained contact with the Polish government-in-exile in London. The AK also collaborated with the Allies, supplying valuable intelligence information, such as the locations and workings of the concentration camps, and the development of the German *Wunderwaffen,* the "wonder weapons."

Noike walked past the damaged cars and crossed the railroad tracks. As he edged down the slope next to the tracks a vast pasture came into view. The land was covered in short grass and wildflowers and dotted with a handful of ancient Oak trees. Two young shepherds were standing near one of the trees, leaning against their shepherd sticks and immersed in conversation. Several feet away from them stood an old man in a German army uniform. Noike led his cows towards the boys and introduced himself.

"*Dzien dobry*, I'm Stasiek," Noike said, still getting used to saying his new name. "I work for the Pyra family."

"Welcome to our pastures!" the first boy said, extending his hand. "I'm Rysiek." He was several inches taller than Noike, with short, dark hair and hazel eyes. Around his neck hung a small wooden cross on a tattered string.

"I'm Jozef," the other boy said, shielding his eyes from the sun.

"Don't mind Franz over there," Rysiek said, pointing at the old man wandering off with his cows. "He's too old to work in the German army so they make him pasture all their cows." The old man was in charge of at least twenty-five cows.

When asked where he came from, Noike told the boys the same story Mr. Huber had told Mr. Pyra: the Ukrainian nationalists had killed his family, who were devout Polish Catholics from Podswientne. It was common knowledge that the nationalists had massacred thousands of Polish Catholics and took over their farms. Nobody asked any questions.

Each morning Noike would take the cows out to the same pastures and spend the day working with the two shepherds. Most of the time the old German soldier would be off on his own, singing the German version of a popular Russian song. He had learned the song when he fought in Russia, somewhere near the Volga river:

> *Volga, Volga our pride,*
> *Mighty stream so deep and wide.*
> *Ay-da, da, ay-da!*
> *Ay-da, da, ay-da!*

Listening to the old man sing one morning, Noike again noticed the wooden cross that hung around Rysiek's neck. He admired it the same way he admired the beggar's bag in Podswientne: it was an object that would legitimize him, keep him safe.

"Rysiek, that's a nice cross you have," Noike complimented him. "I used to have one, but I lost it when I ran away."

"I have another one at home. *Prosze*, take this one," he said, removing his cross and handing it to Noike.

"*Dziekuje bardzo*, Rysiek," Noike thanked his friend as he took the cross.

Tying the cross around his neck, Noike reminded himself that it was all an act, a part he must play to save his life. Though convinced that his God had betrayed him, Noike still feared he would be punished for shedding his name and wearing this religious icon. But what could this God do to him now? His God had taken away his family. He could not imagine a fate any worse than the one left to him.

His new identity was further secured when Mr. Pyra returned from town a few days later and sought Noike out. "Stasiek, I took the liberty of registering you in city hall," he beamed as he handed Noike the papers. "Mr. Huber gave me your date of birth and the names of your family."

In the section for mother it said, "Maria Kwiatkowski," under the section for father it said, "Tomasz Kwiatkowski." Mr. Huber had also provided the names of his fictional brother and sister. No longer was Noike alone in the deceit—his entire family would hide beneath the shroud Mr. Huber had created. The local German officials approved the document and stamped it with a large black swastika. With these papers, few people would dare to question his identity.

Noike tried to fully immerse himself in the role of Stasiek Kwiatkowski, memorizing stories about his fake family, fake home, fake life. But every so often people from his former life would surface, reminding him of his fragile existence. He knew of at least three people from Maciejow who now lived near the Pyras.

One of them was the dog-catcher, a crabby old man who had been feared by every child in Maciejow. Noike used to watch him catch stray dogs with his pole, looping the rope around their necks, then shoving them into a hole in the back of his wagon. The man now lived on Piwna Road, only a few houses away. Noike avoided his house, often taking longer routes to ensure they wouldn't run into each other.

Another person he avoided was the hunchback of Maciejow, a boy a few years older than Noike. He used to tease Noike after school, calling him *Yuda*—a derogatory name for Jews in German. Noike used to think he was saying the word "kernel," like a pumpkin seed kernel, because that's what *Yuda* means in Yiddish. He would shout back *lushpika*, which is the hull of the seed, the garbage. One afternoon when he was driving to the Chelm market, Noike passed the hunchback, who was being pushed in a cart by his mother. Raising the horse reins in the air, Noike managed to block his face and hurry past unnoticed.

The only person he could not avoid completely was Mr. Pietrushka, the wagon driver who had worked for the Maciejow *Gmina*, the town hall, and who had let Noike hold the reins a few times. Mr. Pietrushka moved in with his cousins, who owned the farm next door to the Pyras. One day Noike was working with Zbysiek in the fields when Mr. Pietrushka walked over and asked Zbysiek if he could borrow his wagon to gather firewood. Noike kept his head down until the man left.

A few days later, Mr. Pietrushka showed up at the Pyra farm carrying a large bottle of vodka, a common gift exchanged between farmers. Noike slipped into one of the barns and occupied himself with farm chores. At the dinner hour Marisia called Noike into the house. "I'll be there in a minute—I'm finishing something up," he called back, still afraid to go inside.

It was dark by the time Mr. Pietrushka left the farm. Noike went back into the house and acted as if nothing unusual had happened. Marisia was alone in the kitchen, washing the dishes and cleaning up after dinner.

"Stashi, why didn't you come inside for dinner?" Marisia asked. "Are you angry with me?" "Stashi" was a common nickname for Stasiek. Marisia had grown close to Noike over the summer, often confiding in him about problems she was having with her boyfriend or mother.

"No, I just thought that man was a Ukrainian from Podswientne," he said, suggesting that the man might be connected to the people who had killed his "Polish Catholic" parents. But his concerns were unwarranted, given that the Pyras, too, were Polish Catholic.

"What are you, Jewish?" Marisia asked, softly giggling. The word "Jewish" was said in a quiet voice but it seemed amplified when it reached Noike's ears. *What are you JEWISH?*

"No, I'm not," Noike said, furrowing his brow. "I was just scared of that man."

Marisia nodded her head; she never brought the subject up again.

Noike also slipped when it came to the Polish language. Polish grammar is gender specific: masculine animals use the modifier *dva*, while feminine ones use *dvie*. Noike sometimes confused the two, for example, using *dvie* for bull and *dva* for cow. He also had difficulty with the words used for groups of animals, occasionally formulating convoluted sentences to get his point across.

Eventually Noike improved his Polish grammar and even picked up a few colorful phrases from Mr. Pyra. He learned one of them while struggling to harness one of the horses. The horse tried to chomp on Noike's hands as he shifted the harness left and right. "Ah, Stasiek, don't do it like a Jew," Zbysiek said. He grabbed the harness from his hands and showed him how to do it correctly.

# 26

# THE BOOTS OF SOBIBOR
## Chelm, Poland. Fall 1943

One fall morning a foreign train passing through the pastures slowed down enough for Noike to notice a smartly dressed couple sitting in one of the First Class compartments. The gentleman wore a fine suit and an overcoat; the lady wore a wool coat with a fox collar and a hat topped with a peacock feather. Painted on the side of the train was the word, "Holland."

"What does it mean 'Holland'?" Noike asked Rysiek, not having studied much geography in his first eleven years.

"*Hollandia*," he answered, using the Polish word for Holland. He then drew his hand across his throat and said, *"Do szlachty*, to the slaughter." Rysiek explained that the train was headed for Sobibor, the Nazi death camp located about six miles away. The passengers were among the tens of thousands of Dutch Jews who had been told they would be "resettled" in the East. The smartly dressed couple would have paid extra for the First Class compartment.

Noike looked back at the couple but their car was already beyond the pastures, one step closer to their inevitable deaths. This was the first time Noike understood that Jews were being massacred on a grand scale, that the murders were occurring not only in Poland but throughout all of Europe.

Noike learned more about the train transports when he stepped on a dirt patch a few feet away from the railroad tracks.

"Stasiek, don't stand over there," Rysiek said with a startled look. "A Jew is buried there." Rysiek, like most Poles, was superstitious about stepping on graves.

"What do you mean?" Noike asked, trying not to show concern over the dead Jew.

Rysiek told him about a cargo train that had stopped in the pastures the previous spring. A man inside one of the cars had climbed onto the roof, jumped off, and started running into the pastures. One of the Lithuanian guards, stationed inside a booth on top of another train car, fired several rounds of his machine gun at the man, instantly killing him on the very spot where Noike stood.

A Gestapo officer had come from another part of the train, demanding that the boys find the town mayor. When Mr. Pyra arrived he was told to find some men to bury the Jew. Zbysiek, the Pyras' eldest son, and another young man were called to the scene. They removed the man's clothing and buried him in his underwear. Zbysiek kept his suit; the other man took his boots.

LATER THAT FALL KAZIK, THE YOUNGEST PYRA SON, devised a plan to hitch a ride on one of the trains that bisected their pastures. In his capacity as an engineer at the Chelm train station he was briefed on all of the transports passing through the area; when a train operator told him about a carload of shoes leaving Sobibor for Germany his interest was piqued. That night Kazik waited in the pastures for the train to approach, and when the train slowed to negotiate a bend in the tracks he pushed part of the load into the nearby woods. He planned to keep some for friends and family and sell the rest. Leather shoes were hard to find during wartime.

Zbysiek was responsible for bringing the wagon to the drop-off point and brought Noike along to help. When the two of them arrived Kazik was sorting through the pile, picking out the best ones for his immediate family. Every shape, size, and color imaginable could be found: brown men's wingtips, brightly colored women's pumps, pastel-colored girl's shoes, white baby shoes.

"Stasiek, these should fit you," Kazik said, handing him a small pair of sturdy brown boots that appeared to have belonged to a teenage girl.

"Thank you, Kazik," Noike said, trying to sound appreciative as he took the boots.

In the months that followed, as Noike tied his shoelaces each morning, he wondered about the Jewish girl who had owned the boots: What was her name? What did she look like? Where was she from? Noike imagined that these were her favorite boots, chosen especially for the long journey with her family. He wondered if she was still alive or if the Nazis had already taken her *do szlachty*, to the slaughter. When Noike knelt down to say his prayers, he often thought of the girl and asked her to forgive him for taking her shoes.

A short time after the boot transport Noike saw two young victims with his own eyes. He was standing with the other shepherds when a train stopped in the pastures. The train was for cattle, not passengers, and had barbed wire covering the windows and other exits. Two faces were peeking through one barbed window: a teenage boy and a teenage girl, both with dark hair, dark eyes, and dark expressions; they could have been brother and sister. Noike wanted to tell them that he was one of them, that he wished he could help. But he was afraid to show any signs of emotion, fearing the other shepherds might question his sympathies.

Noike knew these teenagers would be killed but he had no idea how until he met a Polish woman whose brother had been recently released from Majdanek, a concentration and death camp about forty miles away. In contrast to Sobibor, which was located in a densely wooded area, Majdanek was close to the bustling town of Lublin. The Polish woman explained what her brother had observed at the camp: "They take them to showers but they don't give them towels," she said, recounting what the guards had been doing with Jewish prisoners on a daily basis. Few prisoners knew exactly what happened in the showers, they only knew those who entered would never return.

Noike would not come in contact with any Germans officers, except the old shepherd, until members of the local SS division marched into the Pyra house that September. They needed accommodations for a high-ranking SS officer and two of his assistants who planned to stay near Chelm for the next couple of months. They demanded that Mr. Pyra hand over the front half of his home, the same place where Noike was staying.

Noike helped Mrs. Pyra and Marisia move all of their personal belongings out of the two front rooms. Mrs. Pyra swore as they picked up each item and carried it to the other side of the house. Instead of the family of six living in four rooms, they were forced to share just two: the kitchen and the master bedroom. Noike hoped he could keep his distance from the SS officers. He planned to stay in the fields and barns as much as possible.

The high-ranking SS officer was an older man who hardly left the front rooms in the Pyra house. Each day a truck from the military kitchen would arrive with his morning and evening meals. His two assistants, junior officers in their twenties, stood on guard outside. They came from the Battle of Kursk, also called "Operation Citadel," the largest tank battle in history. The

Germans had suffered tremendous losses: more than half a million of their men were killed; thousands of tanks and airplanes were destroyed. A few units had come to Chelm to regroup before they returned to the field.

On first seeing the men Noike's eyes were drawn to the emblem on their hats: the skull and crossbones. They were part of the *Totenkopf* unit, the same unit that had been stationed in Maciejow; the same unit that had led the *aktions* that killed his family. His final days in Maciejow and Luboml suddenly flooded his consciousness. He wanted to flee, but where would he go? He tried to avoid them as much as possible, knowing they would not be there for very long. In his efforts to appear unfazed by their presence, the two junior officers, Franz and Leo, took a liking to Noike.

"*Stanislaw*," they would say, using the German variation of his name and motioning to Noike, "Come over here." He understood most of what they said, given their language's similarities to Yiddish, but he feigned ignorance whenever their entreaties went beyond basic German. He was still in character, playing the role of the young Polish peasant who could not understand much German.

"*Pani mayo?*" the officers would ask. *Pani mayo* means "understand" in Russian. They had learned some Russian during the war and knew many Poles could understand at least a few words.

"*Nix pani mayo*," Noike would respond, using the German word *nix* for no.

For days they would have circular conversations that went nowhere, with Noike saying *nix pani mayo* even when he could indeed *pani mayo*. The officers finally resorted to overt hand gestures and token gifts in their efforts to communicate with Noike.

"*Stanislaw*, have a bonbon," they would say when they received their rations. The fruit-flavored treats looked like lifesavers with their ring shapes and shiny, foil packaging. Noike tried not to stare at the tantalizing candies; sweets of any kind were a rarity during the war. But before long he succumbed to the bonbons and other treats that came with their weekly rations.

Noike's apparent lack of understanding enabled him to overhear conservations not intended for his ears. As he was polishing the senior officers' boots one day, he heard German radio reports citing the number of German prisoners of war from Kursk. Noike paused when they announced the startling number: 300,000 prisoners. The senior SS officer took notice.

"Does he understand German?" he asked the junior officers

"*Nisht*—he only knows how to say '*nix pani mayo*,'" Fritz said, laughing.

Satisfied with the response, the senior officer returned to what he was doing. Noike picked up another pair of black boots and continued polishing.

LATER THAT FALL, ANOTHER SS OFFICER SHOWED UP at the Pyra house, riding a brand new motorcycle with a sidecar lined in dark brown leather. From his post outside one of the barns Noike stole glances at the junior officers admiring the motorcycle and joking with their friend.

"*Stanislaw*, come," the visiting officer said, pointing to the sidecar.

Noike stood there motionless, acting as if he did not understand what the visiting officer had meant. Taking a bonbon every once in a while was one thing, riding into town with an SS officer in uniform was another.

The officer started making sweeping movements towards the sidecar, attempting to illustrate that he wanted to take Noike for a ride on his motorcycle. If Noike declined, it would insult the officer, perhaps make him and the other officers suspicious. At the same time, he was still a little boy, an eleven-year-old boy who had never ridden on a motorcycle.

Noike finally climbed into the sidecar and sat down.

The officer smiled as Noike settled into his seat, then handed him a helmet. "*Stanislaw*, look," the officer said as he put his helmet on. He showed Noike how to close the straps and pointed at him to do the same. And off the two of them went through town: the SS officer with his rifle and bayonet, and the little Jew, in a black sidecar with a freshly-painted swastika plastered along its side.

The visitor left within a few days.

The two junior SS officers had a jeep that was designed to work on road, off road, and on water. Hardly anyone in Chelm owned a car, let alone one that worked on water. One day the officers decided to show off their high-tech vehicle. They drove the jeep to a small pond not far from the Pyra house; it had some fish but it was only a few feet deep. Some locals stood around and shook their heads, watching as the officers drove the jeep into the pond. Although they had no problem getting the jeep into the water, they had to radio for additional help to get it out of the muddy mess.

Towards the end of their stay at the Pyra house, Noike had a chance to ride in this infamous jeep. "Come, *Stanislaw*, we go to the village," one of the junior officers said in German, pointing in the village's general direction. The officers wanted Noike to show them how to get to a small village on the outskirts of town.

As they were driving, Noike overheard the officers' conversation from his perch in the back of the jeep. They were talking about the Polish partisans who were hiding in the woods: "We should probably hide the machine gun," Fritz said to Leo as he was driving. "The partisans will attack if they see it." Although the partisans were well organized and had wide support among Poles, it was still difficult to acquire arms and ammunition. Leo leaned over and slipped the gun under the front seat.

Upon reaching the village Fritz parked the jeep in front of the first farm, a fenced-in property with a few barns and a newly built house painted white. The size and condition of the house suggested that the owners were well-off; many of the neighboring houses were dilapidated, with flimsy roofs and broken fences.

"Stay here, *Stanislaw*," Fritz said as he pointed to the car. The two of them got out and went into the house, carrying a small bottle of gasoline—a rare commodity often traded with farmers in exchange for food. They left the machine gun behind, still tucked under the front seat.

Noike briefly imagined grabbing the gun and spraying the officers with bullets when they emerged from the house. At the same time he knew that killing those two officers could lead to his own death. He was terrified of what the Nazis might do if he was caught. Would they hang him? Shoot him? Send him to Sobibor?

A few minutes later the officers emerged from the farmhouse, Fritz carrying a basket of eggs and Leo a big white pot. Leo lifted the lid on the white pot, pointed inside, and said to Noike, "*Schmaltz, Stanislaw, gut mit brote.* Chicken fat, *Stanislaw*, it's good with bread."

As they drove away, the officers were laughing as they recounted the scene in the house. When they went inside, it was completely empty, yet the stove was still on and the table was set for dinner. The owners must have run away when they saw the SS jeep pull up in front of the house.

The officers continued going house-to-house, collecting eggs, until they had over a hundred of them. When they returned to the Pyra house, Mrs. Pyra was fuming: "Stasiek, where have you been? You were supposed to be—" Mr. Pyra was nice but Mrs. Pyra treated him like her personal servant, asking him to complete an endless number of tasks beyond his farm work.

"*Ruhe, Ruhe, Frau.*" Fritz told Mrs. Pyra to quiet down. "The boy's not finished."

Fritz picked up one basket of eggs and led Noike over to the kitchen sink. He cracked one egg, separated the yolk from the white, dumping each into separate bowls in the sink. He cracked another, then another.

"*Pani mayo, Stanislaw?*" he asked.

"*Pani mayo,*" he replied, nodding his head.

For the next couple of hours, Noike stood over the sink, separating all of the eggs the officers had collected from the farms. He would learn later that they planned to make a German drink called *Eirerlikor*, made from cognac and egg yolks, popular around Christmas time. They gave Mrs. Pyra the egg whites in return for her trouble, more than enough to make a giant stack of angel food cakes. She grumbled as she beat the egg whites, cursing the SS the entire time.

The SS officers moved out of the Pyra house in late October, and headed to a battle taking place around Kiev.

It was a few months later when one of the Pyra's neighbors, a young man by the name of Pawel, asked for a ride to a village several hours away. He worked for the German-controlled electric station in Chelm and needed to replace the generator; apparently there was one available at a flour mill. Since Zbysiek was busy with farm chores, Noike was instructed to drive Pawel.

As Noike neared the designated meeting place the following morning—an intersection near the German barracks—he noticed that Pawel was not alone: a German soldier armed with a rifle and a handgun was walking directly beside him. The soldier climbed into the front seat; Pawel climbed into the back.

"Stasiek, this soldier will be joining us on the trip today," Pawel said, leaning towards the front seat. The soldier was supposed to protect them from Polish partisans who might want to steal the generator.

Noike nodded towards the soldier, trying to contain the fear he felt inside. The two young SS officers at the Pyra house had been cordial but this soldier had piercing eyes and a tight expression on his face; it looked as if he might explode any minute. If Noike slipped up, he feared the soldier would kill him without blinking.

The horses slowly trudged ahead, struggling to carry three passengers. After several hours of driving they hit a muddy patch of road; Pawel and the soldier jumped off and walked alongside the wagon until the conditions improved. Almost two more hours passed before they reached the village of Siedliszcze, where they asked for directions to the flour mill.

"You have to cut through the woods and drive for about a half hour," a Polish farmer explained.

"Ask him if any Polish partisans are in the woods," the soldier instructed Pawel. The soldier could not speak Polish well and relied on Pawel to translate.

Pawel and the farmer conversed in Polish.

"He said daytime is fine but sometimes there are attacks at night," Pawel explained.

The German soldier grabbed the reins out of Noike's hands and started turning the wagon around. In his haste he steered the wagon onto a newly seeded field, destroying weeks of hard work. Noike and Pawel kept silent as the soldier led the horses back onto the road and drove to the center Siedliszcze. As it was already early evening, the street was relatively empty.

"Ask that man where the mayor lives," the officer ordered Pawel, pointing to an old man walking alone on the sidewalk.

A short time later Pawel, Noike, and the soldier were standing outside of the Siedliszcze mayor's front door. "*Aufmachen*," the soldier yelled in German as he pounded on the door.

The mayor, a portly man with thinning black hair, opened the door slightly and peered outside. His pudgy hands trembled as he stared at the German and listened to Pawel translate his orders. The soldier demanded a barn for the horses and a secure place for the three of them to sleep. "Tell him he will be held responsible for our safety," the German added.

The mayor escorted them to the police station across the street, where several policemen were already on duty. The police practically flew out of their chairs when they saw the German soldier walk through the door. The mayor assigned one of them to guard the horses and two others to guard the three visitors as they slept in a room upstairs. One police officer was positioned at the base of the stairs, the other was at the top; both men were armed with machine guns. The windows in the room were covered with thick wire mesh and further secured with sandbags.

"Noike, you should get some sleep," Pawel said, motioning to the narrow bed in the room, which was big enough for one person. "We have a long drive back tomorrow and we need you to be alert."

As Noike lay there trying to fall asleep, the bed suddenly creaked, and someone lay down next to him. Peeling the corner of one eye open, Noike looked to his left and saw the German soldier lying in the bed with his rifle. He immediately started to worry about all of the things that could happen during the night. *What if I have a nightmare and say something in Yiddish? What if I accidentally kick or roll into him? What if he tries to shoot me in the middle of the night?*

Noike forced himself to stay awake all night.

The next morning they drove back to Chelm without the generator. The German soldier was too afraid to encounter the Polish partisans, day or night. He planned to return with a group of soldiers the following day.

As THE WEATHER GREW COLDER, Noike started spending less time out in the pastures and more time on the farm, cleaning the pig stalls and collecting eggs. One day he noticed that one of the female pigs was acting strange: she was rubbing up against him and her backside was flushed. Noike reasoned that she was ready to mate since he had once overheard the Pyra sons talking about animals turning pink when "in heat." The Pyras laughed when Noike shared his observations.

"Stashi, maybe she thinks you're handsome," Zbysiek joked.

"You should look, *Pan* Pyra," Noike said, sticking with his story.

Sure enough, the pig was ready to mate. The Pyras loaded her onto a wagon and brought her to a neighboring farm to mate with a male pig. Farmers were supposed to inform the German army of all livestock births but the Pyras wanted to keep an extra pig for themselves. Instead, they removed the numbered ring from one of their adult pig's ears, and attached it to one of the newborn piglets. They slaughtered the older pig and made kielbasa, salami, bacon, pork chops—more than enough meat to feed the entire family for several months.

Noike had stood nearby during the slaughter. While one man lured the animal over with some food, another dropped a large, wooden sledgehammer over her head. The pigs would normally fall after one swing but this one refused to go down; she started squealing loudly and running around in circles. One of the men had to jump over the fence and give two more heavy swings before she went down.

"Noike, give us a hand," Mr. Pyra called when they were done.

More than three men were required to move the animal to the slaughter area; she must have weighed close to three hundred pounds. One of the men drained the pig's blood and poured it into a vat next to the table. Zbysiek took a small, metal cup off the wall and filled it with some of the blood.

"*Na zdrowie.* To your health!" Zbysiek toasted before taking a small sip. He then passed the cup to the next man, who passed it to Mr. Pyra. Drinking a small amount of the blood was thought to lengthen one's life and increase male virility.

"Noike, take a sip," Mr. Pyra urged, pushing the cup towards him.

"No, thank you, *Pan* Pyra," Noike replied, scared of the drink. If eating pork was a sin, he imagined that drinking the blood would be far worse.

"Ah, be a man, Noike!" Mr. Pyra pressed.

Zbysiek and the other men cheered Noike on.

Wanting to participate in the comradery and prove that he was indeed a man, Noike agreed to take a sip. His hands trembled as he raised the cup to his lips; he tried to ingest as little as possible of the forbidden drink. The thick, mineral taste lingered on his tongue as it oozed down his throat and traveled through his body. He swallowed hard and smiled broadly at the Pyras, overwhelmed with a mixed sense of pride and guilt.

# 27

# FORGIVE ME FATHER
### Chelm, Poland. Spring 1944

It was early spring when Noike started pasturing the cows outdoors again. Over the winter months he had kept the cows closer to home, feeding them with the hay he had collected in the fall. Dozens of mice would scamper away as Noike peeled back each layer of straw; their winter refuge was dismantled by the time spring came along.

In the afternoon the shepherds would take the cows back to their respective farms for milking, then deliver their "milk tax" to the *mlieczarnie*, the milk cooperative operated by the German authorities. The tax amounted to one liter of milk per week for each cow they owned. Noike sometimes visited the Huber house before he went to the *mlieczarnie*.

"Ah, Stashi, you have something for me?" Mrs. Huber would say, knowing exactly what gift he brought.

With a complicit grin, Noike would remove the cap from his milk bottle, revealing a layer of cream that had settled at the top. Gently, he would tip the bottle over, pouring the precious treat into a bowl. Mrs. Huber would add the cream to her baby's bottle, as she had done when they lived together in Podswientne. Although Noike no longer worked for the Hubers he felt an attachment to the family, and would visit them every few weeks.

Continuing on to the *mlieczarnie*, Noike usually ran into one of his fellow shepherds who were also delivering their milk tax. Together they would wait in line behind other farmers and shepherds, then dump their milk into a vat for inspection. The inspectors, typically low-ranking Polish workers, wanted to make sure that the buckets were full and the milk had not been watered down. Anyone who skimped would be punished.

"You need to feed your cow a little better, young man," an inspector warned Noike one day. "The milk looks rather thin today."

"I promise to do a better job from now on," Noike said in earnest. He always tried to ingratiate himself with the inspectors, not wanting to give any of them a reason to distrust or dislike him.

"Stasiek!" Jozef called on his way out of the barracks.

"*Czesc*, Jozef," Noike greeted his shepherd friend.

"Those workers have nothing better to do, eh?"

"They bloody don't! I guess I'll have to keep her out in the pastures longer," Noike joked. He would have to cut back on his special deliveries to Mrs. Huber.

"Well, see you tomorrow, Stasiek," Jozef said as they started going their separate ways. "I have to go to confession or my mother will whip me!"

"Oh, I haven't gone to confession either—I'll go with you," Noike said, wanting to come across as a good Polish Catholic boy. He had overheard the other boys talk about confession but he was unsure what the ritual required of him.

As they were walking to the church Noike posed what he thought was an innocent question: "How do you do confession here?"

"What do you mean?" Jozef shot him a suspicious look. "A Catholic is a Catholic!"

Realizing that his question had sounded absurd, Noike tried to cover his tracks: "Oh, you know, I come from *zabugem*, which is *east* of the Bug River. I thought you might do things different around here." Eastern Poland was considered less sophisticated by western Poland standards; Noike attempted to turn his misstep into a compliment.

"No, it's the same," Jozef said, still wary. "You go to the confession booth and say, 'Forgive me Father for I have sinned,' then do your penance."

"I guess you're right—it's the same way in the east," Noike shrugged, hoping Jozef would forget he had ever asked the question.

"Just follow me and do what I do," Jozef said.

The church was a few miles from the Pyra farm, near the bustling center of Chelm. The gothic style of the building—soaring towers and heavy wooden doors—meant it loomed over all of its neighbors. Larger than life statues of Saint Joseph Calasanz and Our Lady of Mercy stared down at parishioners as they entered the church.

"We need to register over there," Jozef said when they entered the church, pointing to a table manned by the nuns.

"Can you register for me?" Noike asked. "I've never done that."

"All right, I'll be back in a minute," Jozef said.

Noike leaned against the vestibule and took in the unfamiliar surroundings. The walls and ceiling, bathed in the warm afternoon light, were covered in biblical scenes he had never seen before. Older parishioners were standing near one wall, lighting long white candles and whispering prayers. A few younger people were sitting on the wooden pews in the center of the church, their heads bowed and hands clasped in prayer.

"OK, we're both registered," Jozef said when he returned. "I'll go into the confession booth first. When I'm finished, you'll go inside just like I did."

A short time later, Jozef stepped out of the booth and walked up to the altar. Noike inched towards the booth and went inside.

"Forgive me Father for I have sinned," he said as instructed.

"Child, tell me your sins," the priest replied from behind the screen.

*What are my sins?* He asked his God that same question every night as he tried to understand why his family had been killed, why he had lived while others had not. He wondered if this holy sacrament would somehow shed light on the mystery that plagued his thoughts. He wanted an explanation but he was afraid to trust this man of God.

"Child, is something wrong?" the priest asked.

"Father, I didn't act kindly towards Jews," Noike finally said.

The priest turned towards him and remained silent for a moment. Noike realized that he had made a mistake but he kept quiet.

"Are you sorry for what you have done?" the priest eventually asked.

"Yes, Father," Noike said in a soft voice, "I promise not to do it again."

"God the Father of mercies, through the death and resurrection of his Son, has reconciled the world to himself and sent the Holy Spirit among us for the forgiveness of sins; through the ministry of the Church may God give you pardon and peace, and I absolve you from your sins in the name of the Father, and of the Son, and of the Holy Spirit."

Noike left the booth and knelt at the altar. Instead of saying his penance, he silently asked for forgiveness. *Forgive me for entering this house of prayer, forgive me for confessing a lie to that man of God, forgive me for kneeling before this altar.* He wondered if his God was listening to his pleas, if Jewish prayers were even heard anymore.

After the penance, Noike followed the other boys to the communion line. He observed them opening their mouths and the priests placing something inside. When it was his turn, Noike opened wide and accepted the communion, a light crispy wafer. Not knowing what to do with the wafer—whether to eat it and what eating it meant—he kept it on his tongue. Finally, when no one was looking, he bit into the wafer and swallowed.

"Why are you late?" Mrs. Pyra asked when Noike returned to the farm.

"I went to confession," he explained as he sat down for dinner.

"You went to confession?" her face brightened. "Look at Stasiek," she put her hands on her hips as she spoke to her sons. "He goes to confession without being told. Why haven't you two gone?"

A few days later, Jozef suggested that they go swimming in one of the nearby lakes, popular with many boys in the area. At the end of the day, Jozef, Rysiek, and Noike walked to the lake, where they met a couple of other shepherds from a nearby village. One after the other, the boys stripped off their clothes and dove into the lake; bathing suits were not worn in country towns such as this one. Noike sat on the grass near the edge of the water and slowly unbuttoned his shirt.

"Stasiek," one of the boys shouted from the water, "What's taking so long?"

"Nothing," he replied. "I'm coming in!"

Noike had already had one close call on the Pyra farm. He was changing into his pajamas one night when the flap accidentally opened up. Zbysiek had exclaimed: "*Oy aubershnete*. It's cut off!" Noike told Zbysiek that he was drunk, that he didn't know what he was talking about. Zbysiek had appeared embarrassed and did not press further. Aside from that incident, no one had seen Noike naked.

Turning around, Noike removed the rest of his clothing and slowly backed into the water, careful not to let them see the front of his naked body. He swam towards the boys, trying to enjoy the cool water as it enveloped him.

Noike learned to swim in a similar lake in the outskirts of Maciejow, the same one where the white stork appeared every spring. Diving under the water, Noike imagined that he was back in Maciejow, swimming with his brother and sister around the lake. They would sneak up on each other and grab the other's feet. "You can't catch me!" Blima would say in a sing-song voice; she was the fastest swimmer of them all.

When Noike returned to the surface, he saw Jozef lying with his back on the water, urinating into the air. "Who can make their *uryna* go the highest?" he challenged the entire group.

The boys laughed, then started taking turns, shooting their *uryna* into the air, backstroking afterwards to avoid getting hit. Noike knew that his turn would come soon, that it would be impossible to pass without drawing unwanted attention.

He would try to hide his Jewishness.

When his turn came, Noike reached down into the water and pulled his skin forward. Leaning back, he shot his *uryna* into the air, all the time praying that he looked similar enough to the other boys. He then dove under the water, relieved that he had made it through his turn.

But Jozef wasn't finished; he wanted another round.

"I feel cold," Noike said, shivering. "I'm going to get out."

In the days that followed, Noike got the feeling that the other shepherds knew his secret and were talking about him. His conversations with them became less frequent and his eyes were met with silent stares into the distant fields. Towards the end of one of these days, he was left alone in the pastures with Rysiek.

"Stasiek, I don't believe it, but the other boys are talking about you," Rysiek said, with a pained expression. "I think you should leave Chelm right away."

"I understand," Noike responded, not knowing what else to say.

Noike was sorry that his friend felt betrayed. Rysiek had been warm and trusting from the start, often visiting Noike on the Pyra farm after their work, even teaching Noike how to ride a bicycle.

That evening, Noike told the Pyras that the other shepherds were making fun of him and he wanted to leave the farm. Marisia was in tears when she heard the news. She was getting married that Sunday and wanted Noike to be at the ceremony and party.

"Stashi, please stay for my wedding. I want you to take me to church in the *bryczka*." The *bryczka* was an ornately painted carriage with leather seats, used for special occasions such as this one.

"But, Marisia..." Noike tried to protest.

"Please, Stashi, just until Sunday," she pleaded.

Noike agreed to stay for the wedding.

That Sunday morning he took Marisia to the church in the *bryczka*. She wore a floral wreath on her head and a long, white cotton dress, the same one Mrs. Pyra wore for her wedding. When they arrived at the church, Noike helped her from the carriage and promised he would come inside once the horses were tied up. As he steered the wagon towards the back of the church, he spotted Jozef and some other boys walking inside. Fearing one of them might corner him on the way out, he decided to stay with the horses. If the boys came after him, he could escape on the *bryczka*.

*I was always looking for a way out.*

As he sat outside, a wagon driver who was also waiting for someone started asking Noike questions: Why aren't you inside the church? Who do you work for? Where are you from? The questions started to make him nervous, reinforcing his desire to leave the farm, to leave the town as soon as possible.

Marisia finally emerged from the church, walking hand in hand with her new husband, her face blushing, the groom beaming. Noike brought the carriage around and patiently waited as the couple waved to the crowd and their guests pelted them with flower petals. Once they were seated in the *bryczka*, Noike raised the whip and hurried the horses home.

Back at the Pyra house, Noike stood near the barns and watched as the guests arrived, armed with gifts for the young couple.

"Stashi, come inside for some cake!" Marisia called from the house.

"I'll be right there," Noike replied. But once all of the guests were inside, he slipped away and headed into town.

"Stasiek—what a surprise!" Mr. Huber said when Noike showed up at his house. He, too, had grown accustomed to Noike's new name.

Noike stood in their kitchen with a long expression on his face.

"Stashi, is something wrong?"

"I don't like it at the Pyra farm anymore; they're not treating me well," he said. He had been on the farm for almost one year and had voiced some reservations in the past. Mr. Pyra often got drunk and would hurl obscenities at Mrs. Pyra. Although he was never abusive towards Noike, the violent scenes had scared him.

"I understand," Mr. Huber said, pacing the kitchen. "Well, Vanda might know someone in her village who needs a shepherd. Why don't you go over to her house—tell her that I sent you—and she'll introduce you to someone she knows." Vanda was Mrs. Huber's younger sister; the one Noike met back in Podswientne.

Noike followed Mr. Huber's advice and walked to Vanda's home, less than five miles away. Vanda and another girl were preparing dinner when he arrived.

"Stasiek, what brings you here?" Vanda asked, surprised to see him.

"*Pan* Huber said you might know a farmer nearby that needs a shepherd."

Vanda and the other girl began running through the names of all the farmers in the area, trying to figure out which ones might need help this time of year. "Well, the Nowak family has a young boy who already takes care of their cow. The Kaminski family doesn't own a cow. Ah, but, there is a young couple a few miles away who just had a baby. I'm sure they could use your help—they have at least one cow." Vanda gave him their name and explained how to get to the farm.

When Noike arrived at the farm, the owner and his wife greeted him with open arms. "Would you like some *schmetanka* with potatoes?" the wife offered. *Schmetanka* is fresh sour cream, a rare treat for Noike. They set him up with a real bed, a straw-filled mattress—not a makeshift one made from two wooden chairs. This would be the first night in almost two years that he slept on a proper bed.

The next morning Noike took the cow out to the nearby pastures. As he was shepherding the cow, he noticed a wagon with two men slow down, then turn into the pastures. He tried to see if they were carrying guns, worried that the shepherds in Chelm had sent someone to capture him. He was about to run into the fields when he realized it was Mr. Huber and another farmer.

"Come, Stashi!" Mr. Huber waved. "I have another job for you!"

"But I already have a job—I can't leave the cow!" Noike said.

"Don't worry, just come with us," Mr. Huber said.

Most farmers would pay some type of commission for introductions such as this one. Noike later learned that the Pyras often gave Mr. Huber potatoes and grain as a "thank you" for recommending Noike. Chances are that the second farmer was willing to provide a generous "thank you." The first farmer was not under the same obligation, given that Noike had arrived without a formal introduction.

Noike hoisted himself onto the wagon and went with the men to Strahaslov, another small village less than ten miles from Chelm. It was so small that the one road in the village was called Strahaslov Street.

"Broninslaw Szykula, this is Stasiek Kwiatkowski," Mr. Huber did the introductions while the other man drove the wagon. "Broninslaw and his wife recently had a baby girl. They need some help with their cows and the field work."

"Good to meet you, *Pan* Szykula," Noike said.

"Likewise, Stasiek," Mr. Szykula replied stiffly.

Mr. Szykula was a clean-shaven man with cropped dark hair and narrow eyes. He was about the same age as Mr. Huber but not nearly as affable. Anytime Mr. Huber attempted to make conversation, he would simply nod his head, keeping his eyes fixed on the road the entire time.

"Ah, here we are," Mr. Huber said when they reached the farm.

The new farm was much smaller than the Pyra one, with a thatched two-room house and a long wooden barn. Originally part of one large property owned by Mr. Szykula's father, it was now split in two: one half went to Broninslaw; the other to his brother Uzek. The brothers also shared the fields and pastures that lay behind the two houses.

"Well, Stashi, I must return home now," Mr. Huber said, after they had toured the farm together. "Good luck—I know *Pan* Szykula will be pleased with your work."

"*Do widzenia, Pan* Huber," Noike said.

Noike tried to keep some distance from the family and the other shepherds in the village. He went directly home at the end of the day and rarely lingered at the table after dinner. The relationships he had developed in Chelm made him feel more settled, maybe even happy at moments, but they had also put him at risk.

About a week or two into his stay, Noike saw German fighters shooting down a Russian biplane flying over Strahaslov. Rumors spread that the pilot was a Jewish woman who had parachuted from the plane, then killed herself before the Germans arrived at the scene. Noike was intrigued by the story—women pilots were rare, Jewish ones even rarer—but even more excited by its significance. The Russian front was rapidly approaching Strahaslov.

# 28

## BACK TO HIS OWN
*Florida, August 2006*

It was the height of the hurricane season when I returned to Florida later that summer. My parents and I spent our days trying to stay dry, shuttling between the house, restaurants, and the local shopping mall. One afternoon my father and I camped out in the living room and talked about the time he spent in Chelm.

"Did the kitchen stove provide some warmth in the winter?" I asked, like a concerned parent. Sleeping on two kitchen chairs for an entire year sounded awful; I prayed the room was at least warm.

"Sure, a little," he said, sensing my concern. "Do you want to see the stove?"

My father left the room and returned with photos from his trip to Chelm in 1991. He had reconnected with the Pyras through a business associate in New York who had contacts in Poland. The Pyras were pleased when they learned that little Stasiek was coming for a visit.

"Here's one of Zbysiek," my father said, holding up a photo of a stooped older man in a crumpled cardigan. "Here's one of my pastures—it used to be all grass but now they farm cabbage and other vegetables. And, here's the stove," he said, setting down a few close-ups of his former sleeping quarters. The chimney was white-washed, like the outside of many homes in the region, while the base was covered in bright white tiles. Stacks of dented pots and pans were piled on the burners. The chairs weren't there anymore.

"Mr. Pyra and his wife were dead by then?"

"Mr. Pyra, Mrs. Pyra, and Kazik were all killed in a terrible car accident in the late '50s. Zbysiek took me to visit their graves at the cemetery."

Marisia was still alive but she recently moved into a nursing home. Zbysiek discouraged my father from seeing her—he said she wouldn't remember him—but my father had insisted. He was carrying a tremendous bouquet of flowers when he entered Marisia's room at the home. "Remember me?" he asked, leaning over to give her a big hug.

Her beautiful blonde hair had turned gray; her clear blue eyes were now cloudy. She had a distant look on her face, seemingly unaware that my father had entered the room. My father thought it might have been too late, but suddenly her youthful glow returned: "Stashi, I remember you—*ty mnie kochal,* you loved me!"

"Did you tell the Pyras you were Jewish?" I asked.

"No, I didn't. My Polish contacts in New York told them I was Jewish and explained what had happened to my family," he said.

During that visit my father also went into the town of Chelm to see the former synagogue, *Beit Hamidrash*. He had always wanted to visit the synagogue when he lived in Chelm but was afraid to show any interest. He made it to the entrance but could not bring himself to go inside. A few years ago it was turned into a pub and banquet hall selling German beers. Cheap plastic banners advertising Heineken beer were strung across the doorway.

On the way back to the house they drove past the Polish Catholic church my father had attended while living on the farm. A large crowd of people were gathered near the entrance, dressed in their Sunday best.

"Would you like to go inside?" Zbysiek asked, slowing the car down.

My father nodded, curious to revisit another part of his former life.

The inside of the church appeared as he remembered but it had been renovated in recent years: the old murals had been cleaned; the pews and floors had a fresh coat of polish. The priest was standing at the altar leading a prayer in Polish. Suddenly, all of the parishioners dropped to their knees and bowed their heads in prayer. My father was the only person who remained standing, a modest protest for all of the times he could not stand, for all the times he could not be honest about his faith.

When they left the church, Zbysiek turned to my father and said: "I see you went back to your own."

# 29

# AWAKENED FROM A DEEP SLEEP
### Strahaslov, Poland. Summer 1944

Instead of cowering inside like most people in the village, Noike and the other Strahaslov shepherds were eager to get a good look at the battle between the Russians and Germans. One afternoon they watched a Russian plane circling above the German base. The red star on the wing darted back and forth, teasing its target. Suddenly, the plane revved up its engine and dove down to attack. The German soldiers on the ground fired back, riddling the plane with a stream of bullets, sending it crashing into their ammunition warehouse. Within seconds, flames erupted from the warehouse, debris flew hundreds of feet in either direction. The boys covered their heads and ran into a ditch, lying still until the explosions stopped.

As the fighting intensified over the next few weeks, the other shepherds finally gave into their parents' demands and stayed close to home while the village was under attack.

"Stasiek, I think you should keep the cow near the house," Mr. Szykula said one morning. "The fighting has gotten much worse—you could get injured out in the pastures."

"*Pan* Szykula, there's no need to worry, I'll be fine," Noike said, flushed with bravado. "I'll stay close to the woods where they won't be able to see me."

Noike rejoiced in the battle; he did not want to miss one moment.

He was pasturing the cow near the woods a few days later when a Russian plane flew into the area and hovered above the pastures. The plane started firing in his direction, perhaps thinking that Noike was part of the AK, *Armia Krajowa*, the Polish partisan group. Now that the Germans were almost defeated, the AK was trying to reestablish the Polish state. But the Russians had other plans: they wanted to incorporate Poland into the Soviet Union and install a communist style government.

Grabbing the cow by its chain, Noike raced into the woods. The plane tried to follow him as he ran deeper and deeper into the forest. Craning his neck back, he looked up into the sky, watching as the tiny form continued to dart back and forth. Ten, maybe fifteen minutes later, he heard the plane engine roar as the aircraft turned around and left, in search of another target. As Noike emerged from the woods he discovered dozens of bullet casings littering the ground. After surviving the *aktions* in Maciejow and Luboml and living in the same house as the SS, he realized it was foolish to risk death at this stage. Liberation could be weeks or even days away. He finally agreed to pasture the cows closer to home.

Although Noike was near the farm, he was still able to observe much of the battle. The German troops in Strahaslov had built a trench right behind Mr. Szykula's house. They would set up their massive machine gun at one end of the trench, fire at the Russian planes, then run to the other end and shoot additional rounds. They hoped the enemy would think they had more men, when in fact a large number had been decimated. Word spread that the Russians had already defeated the German army in Chelm.

During this time a group of German soldiers moved into the front half of the Szykula house. These men were fanatics, diehards who refused to give up, even knowing that their days were numbered with the Red Army advancing from the east and the Allies from the west.

The unit commander was the only one who slept in the house, but each night a group of the soldiers would come inside to wash up. Noike had been able to avoid any direct communication with them, except the night when a group showed up while their commander was out in the field. The Szykulas and Noike, who were now sleeping in the same room, heard the men enter the house. None of them dared to move.

"Where's the water?" one of them shouted from the front room.

"Stasiek, *prosze*, go help them," Mr. Szykula urged. He, too, was afraid of the soldiers. "Give them whatever they want."

Noike stepped into the front room, which was dark except for an oil lamp sitting on one of the desks, illuminating the framed photo of Hitler that hung above. Some of the soldiers were standing around the desk and a few others leaned against the walls. Their faces were blackened with soot; only the whites of their eyes could be seen in the darkness. Strapped across their chests were row upon row of ammunition, bullets and hand grenades that could blow Noike to pieces in seconds.

"What are you staring at, boy?" one of the men barked in German.

"Where's the water?" another demanded. "*W-o-d-a*," he said again, this time enunciating each letter in Polish.

Noike led the soldiers to the kitchen, where they kept a barrel full of water. He pulled a chair over and reached into one of the cupboards, handing them a loaf of bread, biscuits, and whatever else struck their fancy.

"*Danke*, young man," one of the more senior men said, mussing up Noike's hair. The group reconvened in the front room, then stormed back out of the house and into the dark night.

Noike returned to the bedroom and crawled into bed. As he lay there, he thought back to the time in Maciejow almost three years ago, when the SS officer had placed the gun against his forehead and had asked him about his "sisters" in the house. He felt the same relief that overcame him when the SS had left that night, but something was different, something inside him had changed. Back then he had much to lose; now there was nothing.

Less than a week later, on a Sunday morning, the Red Army started shelling Strahaslov. Noike watched the puffs from the artillery fired in Chelm, then heard shells whistling overhead before they exploded in the distance. Straw roofs flew through the air in flames, landing blocks away from their original homes, charred beyond repair.

"Everyone, down to the basement," Mr. Szykula instructed his family. There were now at least ten people huddled in the main room; his brother, Uzek, and his family had come from next door for shelter.

Noike followed the two families down the stairs into the basement.

The Szykulas cowered close together, praying their homes would not be destroyed. The brothers were trying to calm their wives; their wives were trying to calm their children. Noike was living the dream he had waited for all these years: he would finally be liberated from the Germans. In the midst of the shelling and hysteria, somehow he fell into a deep sleep.

The basement was empty when Noike opened his eyes. The sound of shelling was replaced by the sound of heavy trucks. Running out into the street, Noike saw the Red Army rolling through the village, escorting about one hundred German soldiers, their hands stretched high into the air, defeated. Many of the villagers lined the street, some blankly staring, others cheering as their former occupiers were marched away.

Noike ran back into the house, to the front room, where the German commander had been stationed. He stood on a chair, then climbed on top of the desk. Reaching up, he lifted the portrait of Hitler off the wall and smashed it to the floor. The glass cracked in a few places, but the photo was still inside the frame, barely scratched. Stepping down from the desk, he went over to the picture and pounced on the glass with his bare feet. Shards of glass flew in all directions; small pieces pierced the soles of his feet. He felt no pain as he pulled the picture out of its frame and tore it to shreds.

# 30

## THE AVENGER
*New York. Circa 1980*

"Six million Jews, Hitler killed," my father would say.

"Hitler *vas meshugener*, a madman," my maternal great aunt would say.

"Six brothers and sisters, I had. Hitler killed all of them," my great uncle would add, his eyes downcast.

As I grew older, the adults began to speak more freely about the war, at least among themselves. Who was this Hitler person? I wondered. If he was so terrible, why didn't someone kill him? If he managed to kill six million Jews, why couldn't we kill just one of him? But no one had done it. No one had done it, and that's why my aunts, uncles, grandparents, and millions of others had been killed.

Going back in time to save my father and his family suddenly felt less heroic; my father's other relatives, neighbors, and millions of Jews across Europe would still be in danger. If I wanted to help everyone, if I really wanted to make a difference, I had to get Hitler out of the picture.

One night, after my father had kissed me good night and closed my bedroom door, I decided to change my time travel course. Instead of flying to Maciejow, I would head to the heart of Germany, where I assumed Hitler was headquartered.

As I soared through the sky, the world around me changed from color to sepia, and then to black and white. Zipping open my pajamas, I tossed them aside, revealing my corduroy jumpsuit and cowboy boots, polished especially for this occasion.

Over Nazi headquarters I spotted a dim light streaming from an office deep in the compound. Pointing my cowboy boots down towards the earth, I slowly descended, landing outside the office door.

The hallway was cold and deserted.

Pressing my ear against the door, I listened for signs of life. Silence.

Pressing my ear again, harder, I made out the faint sound of writing—rapid writing—followed by the slamming of book covers. Every few minutes there would be a pause, then what sounded like a pen being thrust into an inkwell.

Gently, I knocked on the door.

"Come in," an accented voice replied.

I turned the knob and pushed the door open, letting in a tremendous gust of wind.

Hitler was sitting alone at his desk, hunched over stacks and stacks of notebooks, illuminated by one light bulb hanging overhead. The rest of the room was shrouded in darkness. He was scrawling in one of the notebooks, making revisions to his master plan, counting how many Jews he planned to kill. The pages in the book fluttered as I stood in the doorway.

Hitler looked up from his notebook, down at his watch, and then back at me: "Little girl, what are you doing here? Isn't it past your bedtime?"

The door flew shut, but the wind refused to leave, whipping Hitler's papers all about the room. He reached left and right, trying to grab the papers before they drifted out the window.

"It's because of you that my father lost his childhood; it's because of you that I didn't have a full set of grandparents, aunts, uncles, and cousins," I said, pulling a Luger out of the right pocket of my jumpsuit; it was the same type of gun the SS had pointed at my father.

"Now, now, little girl," he said, trying to calm me down. "Don't get so excited. What's your father's name? I'll make sure no one hurts him." He grabbed one of his notebooks and began to scan the names.

"You have to let all of them go—you can't hurt any of them," I said, stomping my cowboy boot on the cement floor.

"That's impossible. And why do you care about all of those other people?" he asked, nonchalantly waving his hand through the air.

"Put both your hands back on the desk," I ordered him.

Looking into his evil eyes, I knew instantly that he would be unstoppable. Killing him was the only way to put an end to his plans. As I considered where to fire the bullet, it occurred to me that killing him also meant my parents might not emigrate to the United States, that they would never meet. If they didn't meet, I would never be born—I would never exist.

I pondered this fact as I looked into Hitler's eyes.

"Little girl, have you come to your senses?" He smiled weakly; a thick layer of sweat had formed above his mustache.

"I'm not a 'little girl,'" I said, walking closer to him, pressing the gun against his forehead.

He looked up into my blue eyes, which were piercing through every inch of his being.

"It's you—" he started to say, but I pulled the trigger.

Standing over him, I watched in slow motion as the bullet burrowed its way into his head, into his *meshugener* brain. His body fell back into the chair. Blood poured from the wound, dripping onto the floor. As his breath slowed, my body began to fade away, starting with my fingertips, then working its way to my arms, legs, torso and face. With his final breath, I ceased to exist, but now many others would live.

# 31

# SOMETHING GOOD

*Strahaslov, Poland. Summer 1944*

Eager to learn more about the German defeat, Noike left Strahaslov and headed for Chelm. Walking along the main road he came upon a column of Russian soldiers marching into town. One of the young soldiers made eye contact with him.

"Sir, can you help me?" Noike asked him in Russian, "I'm Jewish, I want to go home."

"Where are you from?" the soldier asked.

"Maciejow—it's near the towns of Luboml and Kovel," Noike explained.

"Don't go there, son, they'll kill you," the soldier warned.

*They still want to kill me?* The war was almost over, he had been liberated, yet it was still unsafe? Hardcore Banderites, he soon learned, were still determined to establish an independent Ukrainian state, free of Poles, Russians, and Jews. They were holed up in the woods, attacking Russian soldiers and Jews who tried to return home.

"Some Jews have gathered in a safe house near the old synagogue in Chelm. I suggest you go there—they might be able to help you."

Noike thanked the soldier before venturing towards the house.

Along the road Noike saw dead German soldiers, their bodies rotting in the thick summer heat. One of them had a cherry sized hole in his helmet that was oozing with blood. Noike felt a strange satisfaction as he passed this corpse and the many others lying prostrate in the wheat fields.

When he reached the safe house he found it filled with dozens of Jews who had surfaced from hiding places in the surrounding woods, farms, and villages. Crowded into one small room was also a group of Russian Jews who had escaped from Sobibor. They had been serving in the Red Army when they were captured by the Germans in '41.

"Sit with us, young man," one of the former soldiers beckoned Noike. He sat with the men and listened to stories about their escape from Sobibor.

"One of the high-ranking SS officers, he wanted me to make him a suit," one of the more senior men said. He had been a tailor before the war broke out, retained by the Germans for his superior skills.

"We made an appointment to fit the suit—the *same time every day*!" He pounded his fist after each word for emphasis. "Meanwhile, many other craftsmen were making similar appointments, and another group was securing weapons."

One of the men involved in the escape, Shlomo Szmajzner, had stashed away about a dozen axes used by the lumber brigade. Another man, Leon Feldhendler, had taken hundreds of knives from one of the storage rooms: pocket knives, Dutch switchblades, Jewish ceremonial knives. All these knives had been confiscated from Jews killed at Sobibor.

"Then, one day," the man continued, "when the time was right, we arranged for a special fitting for that SS officer."

The other men looked at one another, nodding, remembering that fine moment.

"We killed that son of a bitch and ten other of those SS butchers. As we stormed the gate, we also got our hands on those Ukrainian bastards who had blindly followed their orders."

Three hundred of them managed to escape; fifty survived the war.

Noike listened in awe to these men—Jewish men—who had managed to rebel against the enemy, to kill the most evil of killers. He thought their stories must be fiction, not believing that any Jews had survived Sobibor. It was not until several years after the war, when he read several eyewitness accounts from Sobibor, that he learned the stories had indeed been true.

Noike considered staying in the safe house but the living conditions were poor: there was little food or water, the rooms were overcrowded, and many people were sick from disease or exhaustion. Assuming that Jews were no longer in danger—at least in Chelm—Noike thought it would be safe to visit the Pyras. He especially wanted to see Marisia, having always felt guilty about leaving on her wedding day.

Noike heard a familiar voice as he was heading towards the Pyra farm: "Stasiek?" Turning around he discovered Mr. Pyra's sister, who had visited the farm several times while he was living there.

"Where have you been? The Pyras were worried about you," she said.

"I've been living in Strahaslov but I'm going to visit them now," he explained.

"Don't go there now—it's too dangerous," she warned.

Noike later learned that the Pyras were running a Polish underground cell associated with the AK, *Armia Krajowa*, the Polish partisan group. The Russians were questioning them, trying to determine if they had collaborated with the Germans, or if they supported the Russian cause.

Where should he go now? Without many alternatives, Noike found himself returning to the farm in Strahaslov, where he would at least have a roof over his head, steady work, and food on the table. His absence that day would go unnoticed—there was too much commotion after the shelling and liberation.

The next day he resumed his responsibilities on the farm. He still pastured the cow in the mornings but spent most afternoons out in the fields. The summer harvest had begun and additional hands were hired to manage the extra work. One man would cut the wheat while Noike followed close behind, bundling the sheaves with pieces of straw. As he was forming a bundle one morning, a young girl who was helping with the harvest ran into the fields.

"Stasiek—your aunt is here!" she said.

*My aunt? Which aunt?*

"Something good is not for long," Mr. Szykula said with tears in his eyes, worried that he would lose his prize worker during the busy season.

Noike felt no obligation to the farmer. One of the other shepherds had told him that Mr. Szykula reported a Jew he had found hiding in his haystack early on in the war. Before the Germans came to arrest the man, Mr. Szykula demanded that he hand over his leather boots. Death was certain for the Jewish man, most likely at Sobibor.

"Did she say her name?" Noike asked. "What was her name?"

"I don't know," the girl shrugged her shoulders. "She's waiting near the woods with someone from town."

Noike did not believe that anyone from Maciejow had survived, let alone one of his relatives. Dropping the wheat to the ground, he left the fields, following the same path the girl had taken.

Walking towards the road, Noike made out Mr. Huber and a young woman wearing a *babushka* over her hair. As he got closer, he realized it was his aunt Fania, the middle sister of his three paternal aunts. He now wondered about his two other aunts; he now wondered about everyone.

"Noikele!" Fania cried, before launching into an exhaustive story in Yiddish.

He had not heard or spoken his mother tongue in almost two years but he could make out most of what she said. Sabina, the eldest of the three aunts, had fled to Russia a few months ago and was now in Niezin working at a sugar factory; she was trying to get travel documents to return to Poland. Fania had not received word about his other aunt, Hanka, nor anyone else.

Fania was working on a farm owned by Polish Czechs for most of the war. When she learned that Maciejow was liberated, she went back in search of family and friends. Finding no one, she continued traveling west, and soon heard that many Jewish survivors were gathered in Chelm. She was passing through Chelm when she ran into the gardener's wife, Elizabeta, from Maciejow. Elizabeta introduced Fania to Mr. Huber, who then took her to the farm in Strahaslov.

"Are you all right?" Fania asked him. "I have *schmetanka* back at the house—you loved *schmetanka*!" She worried as she looked down at her young nephew: his feet were cut from working the fields barefoot; he had difficulty looking her in the eyes; he seemed more comfortable speaking with the Polish farmers.

"*Tak*," he replied in Polish, nodding his head. He was still unable to speak the forbidden language, to form the unfamiliar words.

He had convinced himself many times that his old world would never return. When parts of it began to resurface he was in disbelief, conflicted, confused. He had moved back and forth between his old world and the new one, but at some point he had unknowingly succumbed to the new one. He had forgotten how to talk like a Jew, eat like a Jew, worship like a Jew. No longer was he playing a part: he had *become* a Polish farm boy; he had become Stanislav Kwiatkowski.

As the three of them walked away from the farm, his mind drifted off as he considered what it would be like to play his new role: Noike, an orphaned Jewish boy, twelve years old.

## 32

# FREEDOM TRAIN
*Florida, Fall 2006*

"I ordered sunny weather for you this week," my father said as we drove away from the airport. The rainy season had finally started winding down; rays of sun were peeking through the late afternoon clouds.

"Great—maybe we can actually go to the pool this time!" I said.

My father and I agreed to take a break from interviews and writing for a while. There was still more to learn about his experiences, but doors had been opened; so much had already been gained. Now I knew where he came from, where my aunts, uncles, grandparents, and great grandparents came from. My *Baba* Pesel was no longer just a sepia-colored photo in a lacy gold frame; she was a strong, courageous woman who raised three children on her own and managed to save one from the largest massacre of the twentieth century. My *Tante* Blima and Uncle Herschel had also come alive; it was as if I had truly known them.

"You might want to take a look at those boxes from New York," my father said when we arrived at the house. "They're in the back of the guest room closet."

At the end of every year, I would stuff all sorts of schoolwork into giant black garbage bags: composition notebooks; homework assignments with gold stars; art projects like my Thanksgiving turkey drawing. Sometimes I worried that I had kept too many things, but my father would always alleviate my concerns: "You don't have to throw anything out—whatever you want to keep, we'll put it in the attic!" He would then take the bags from me, climb up to the attic, and place them next to the bags he had stowed away for my brother and sister. Over the years it would become impossible to crawl more than a couple of feet into the attic, yet the space was as big as our four-bedroom house. After college, I whittled my garbage bag collection down into six cardboard boxes, and wrote the word "KEEP" across the side of each one.

They sat idle until my parents moved to Florida.

I went over to the guest room closet and dragged some of the boxes out.

Digging into the first box, I found an assortment of photos taken in the second decade of my life: dozens of college ones, still in the envelopes from the print shop; travel ones from Asia hastily placed in temporary photo albums. Between the photos were bundles of letters, held together with rubber bands on the verge of disintegration, the last vestiges of my life before email. The second box had much older letters, photos, and other random pieces of ephemera. Many of the items were not even mine; they were from my father's closet in New York.

"Dad, some things in those boxes belong to you," I said, walking into his office.

"Oh, yeah," he looked up from his desk. "What do you have there?"

"Do you remember this little book from Bremen?" I held up a two-inch by two-inch accordion book with black and white photos of various sites: a windmill, a Gothic church, a dock, a lighthouse.

"I probably bought that before I left for the United States," he said.

A little more than two years after he was liberated, my father boarded a boat in Bremen, Germany, and set off for New York City. The United Children's Committee sponsored the voyage, sending hundreds of orphans from all over Europe. His three paternal aunts—Fanian, Sabina, and Hanka—would join him in the United States within a few years.

"What about this postcard of the 'Freedom Train'?" I asked. "Did you take this train when you arrived in the United States?"

"No, I bought that many years later," my father said, laughing at my naïve question. "After they registered us at Ellis Island, we had to take a ferry over to Manhattan."

All of the children were transferred to a makeshift orphanage until further arrangements could be made for them. Within a few days, my father's Aunt Hinda, his paternal grandfather's sister, located him and brought him to her home in Brooklyn; other survivors had informed her about his arrival. Hinda emigrated from Luboml to the United States in the 1930s. My father lived with her until he married my mother.

"And how about this Brooklyn bus transfer?" I asked. The transfer, a slightly yellowed slip of paper in otherwise perfect condition, afforded the holder a ride on Route B-39 over the Williamsburg Bridge.

"It must have been from a special trip," he grinned. "Maybe I had a date and kept the transfer as a memento."

As my father reflected back to the mysterious date, I pictured the little boy, already a gangly teenager, boarding a Brooklyn bus for his special night out, filled with optimism and the realization that he was finally free.

*Drama club in Maciejow. Noike's father is on the floor, far left; his mother is sitting in the middle of the second row.*

*Kindergarten in Maciejow, Poland. Noike's sister is in the front row, 6th from right with eyes closed.*

*Faige Ginsburg's (Noike's cousin) engagement party in Luboml, Poland, circa 1938.*

*Dedication of Hebrew School in Maciejow. Noike's father is on the far left, holding the tray.*

## ACKNOWLEDGEMENTS

I'm grateful to those who subjected themselves to my early drafts: Michelle Orange, Elizabeth Bernstein, Greg Roensch, Ali Oshinsky, Marilyn Fefer, Pamela Walshe and Pia Chatterjee.

I'm also indebted to Nicole Celichowski for not only reading one of my early drafts but for designing a series of beautiful book jacket designs. There are at least seven other directions that are as brilliant as the one you see on this final version.

And, most important, thanks to my dad, Leon Ginsburg, for sharing his stories with me when I was a little girl and throughout our 2006 interviews. Having them written down means my daughter, her children, and many others will not forget all of the Jews who perished in Maciejow, Poland and its environs.

www.ingramcontent.com/pod-product-compliance
Lightning Source LLC
Chambersburg PA
CBHW020927090426
42736CB00010B/1065